GASTROANOMALIES

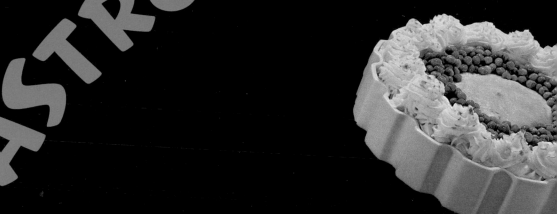

Also by James Lileks

Mommy Knows Worst

Interior Desecrations

The Gallery of Regrettable Food

GASTROANOMALIES

QUESTIONABLE CULINARY CREATIONS FROM THE GOLDEN AGE OF AMERICAN COOKERY

James Lileks

CROWN PUBLISHERS
NEW YORK

Published in the United States by Crown Publishers,

an imprint of the Crown Publishing Group, a division of Random House, Inc.,

New York. www.crownpublishing.com

Crown is a trademark and the Crown colophon is a registered

trademark of Random House, Inc.

Library of Congress Cataloging-in-Publication Data is available upon request.

ISBN 978-0-307-38307-5

Printed in the United States of America

Design by Maria Elias

10   9   8   7   6   5   4   3   2   1

First Edition

Dedicated to the readers of lileks.com and all the
fine folks who contributed to the site. This book is also
dedicated to everyone who couldn't bear to throw that silly
old cookbook away because "it might be useful someday."
They were right, and here's the proof.

Contents

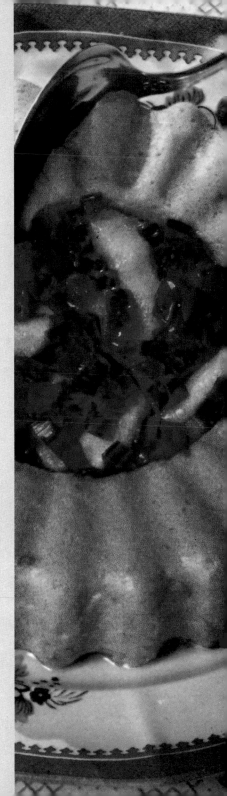

Introduction

Every old cookbook is a scrapbook of all-American joys. The hearty simple dishes remind you of special family meals. The silverware, the plates, the tabletop accessories in the pictures—each little detail recalls things you saw when you were nine, dressed in your best, having holiday supper. The hairstyles and typefaces point back to a pure perfect era when everything was "keen." Everything was "neat." Then you turn the cookbook page and find a recipe for Brains in Thyroid Juice, and you remember: Oh, right.

Those were the days when people ate glands and tongues and jellied calf retinas and minced eel and toad toes in aspic and God knows what else. Those were the days when "Chinese" meant crunchy noodles from a can, "Mexican" meant three entire grains of pepper added to a gallon of tomato juice, and pizza crusts were fashioned from hand-pounded saltine crackers dusted with the breath of someone who'd recently said the word "oregano."

These were the good old days, in other words. The recipes from this golden age of culinary creations are literally heart-warming: Take one heart, slice, fry in oil, serve warm.

The examples found herein are cruel and unfair, of course. It's not the fault of the chefs that the photographers made the alfredo sauce look like Elmer's Glue. Half these dishes might be edible, if consumed in a low-light environment. Just because the modern palate shies away from things like "Lard-Stuffed Deep-Fried Lard Logs" doesn't mean they didn't taste fine, in a lardy sort of way. Just because we eat less rabbit now doesn't mean rabbit didn't make a fine cold sandwich meat, particularly when salted and slathered with mayo. People enjoyed their meals in the bygone days. To mock those tastes now because we think we're so cool—well, that's the height of smug, retrospective condescension.

It is also fun, which is why this book exists.

Bon Appétit!

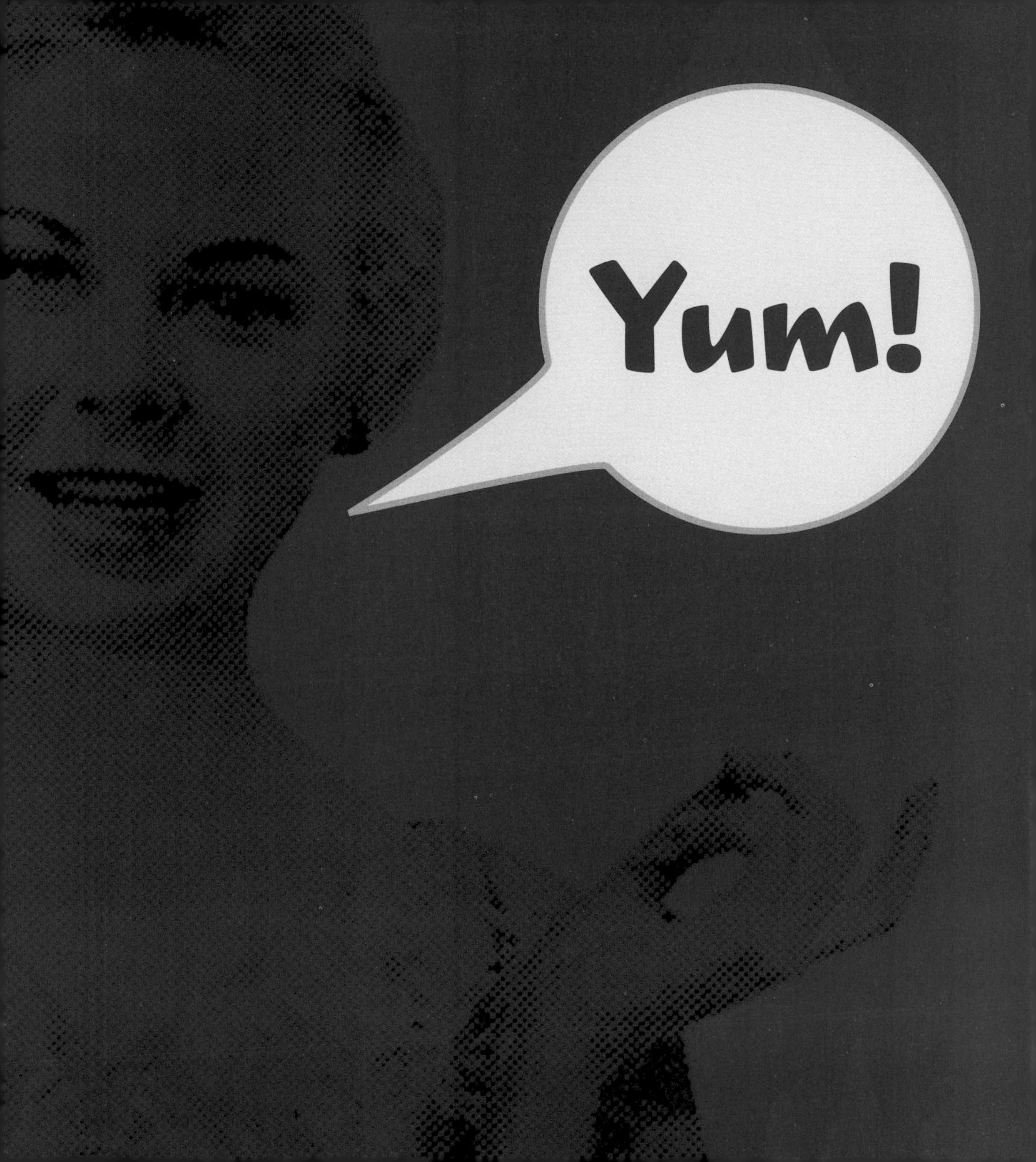
Yum!

Begin the Day with Chicken Fetuses and Pig Slices

* * ★ * *

We start with the most important meal of the day: breakfast! It's the one meal in which you've permission to eat things in quantities and combinations you'd otherwise avoid. People consider a plate of pancakes and bacon to be a perfectly acceptable morning meal, but if you eat a stack of bread drenched in corn syrup with strips of fried pig fat for supper, people might think you've lost your mind. *Poor fellow. He thinks that's dinner.* With every other meal you feel obligated to have a salad, as if to atone for your caloric sins; the only thing green at the breakfast table is a sprig of parsley, which sits there like a diplomat from a nation with which the omelet has a tense relationship.

A good breakfast is a wonderful treat and remarkably hard to ruin, and the recipe books of the past generally left it alone. That's not to say they didn't try.

Cock-a-doodle don't, okay?

These eggs resemble creamed bile with mustard sauce, and the ubiquitous White Fluid makes it impossible to eat this with your hands. The meat's nice and clammy, but really: Is there enough fat in this dish? If your corpuscles don't have to go single-file through your major arteries, you can still indulge a little more. Have two!

Now---
our day starts out *right* with the EVEREDY

Bacon-Egger*

This brand-new utensil is full of brand-new features! Fries bacon flat, dries it hot while you fry your eggs! Place cover plate **(1)** on top of bacon. Bacon fries *flat*—no turning, no splattering! Drippings run into ring-drain **(2)**. Slide cooked bacon onto *hot* warming and drying apron **(3)**. Fry 3 to 4 eggs in drippings left in "dished" center. Pour out drippings through pouring slot **(4)**. Wash Bacon-Egger like glass or china. NO SCOURING NEEDED. You can buy this new gift-boxed utensil at department, house furnishing or hardware stores.

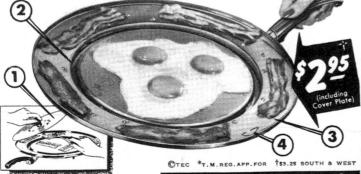

$2.95
(including Cover Plate)

©TEC *T.M. REG. APP. FOR †$3.25 SOUTH & WEST

Show your dealer this advertisement—he'll sell you a genuine Bacon-Egger . . . or write us.

The EVEREDY Co.
EAST STREET · FREDERICK, MD.
MAKERS OF 'TATER BAKER · OVENOLA · KAKE-SAVER

The process involved with the Bacon-Egger looks slightly less complicated than a military invasion. *Cover bacon! Observe drippings running through ring drain! Reposition bacon to secondary staging ground, deploy eggs! Vacate excess animal fluids through designated Slot 4!* The illustration clearly doesn't help, since Wifey seems to be heading past Hubby to throw the ungodly mess out, not serve it. Unless he has a habit of pulling up a chair between the stove and the breakfast table just to keep an eye on her.

The Everedy Co. also made the Tater Baker, the Ovenola and the Kake-Saver, three household items that established a direct connection between usefulness and peculiar spelling. Some failed Everedy products may have included the Spag-a-Drano, the Bred-B-Fresch, and the Ev-R-Sharp Mohelola, a combination carrot peeler/infant circumciser.

They want waffles, do they? Well, fine!

They want me to crack the eggs, pick out the shells, make the batter, haul out the waffle maker, throw away the imperfect ones that have deformed edges like amputee stumps, collect the perfect square ones and serve them all at the exact same temperature because GOD forbid one should be cold even though I can't make more than four at a time and I have to serve five people at a time. Is that what they want? Waffles?

Well, they didn't say what they wanted on top of the waffles, did they?

Oh, you wanted syrup? You should have said something. You should have practiced saying "syrup." It's a hard word, like "please" and "thank you."

The Plus *FOOD* For *Minus* MEALS

Best FOR COOKING — Page 1

Best FOR MIXING — Page 13

Best AS A CEREAL — Page 16

As a piece of design, this late-thirties brochure is a tidy little masterpiece. It makes a nice connection between "food" and "meals." The only problem? You have *no* idea what the thing's about.

As you probably didn't surmise, this booklet concerns the wonderful effects of bran. According to the book, Depression-era foods are often bran-minus and thus need a breakfast bran-boost to provide you and your family with dense and dependable defecation. Let's turn the page and take a look at how it works, shall we?

For Sunny Living, Choose Any of These Delightful Ways to Use Kellogg's ALL-BRAN

In waffles, with other cereals, or in salads

As a cereal with milk or cream

In muffins, breads or cookies

514

Printed in U.S.A.

BEST AS A CEREAL

The "bulk" content of Kellogg's All-Bran is higher than that of any other common food. It definitely corrects the "bulk-minus" meal—the most frequent cause of constipation.

When common constipation due to "bulk-minus" meals does occur, your family begins to feel under par—not exactly sick, but certainly not well. Avoid this condition by serving All-Bran regularly for regularity.

Try All-Bran as a cereal with milk or cream—two tablespoons daily will give you the "bulk-plus" meals so necessary in the well-balanced diet. In chronic cases, with each meal. All-Bran is much more effective than part-bran products. Sold by all grocers. Made by Kellogg in Battle Creek, Michigan.

The Martians have conquered the Japanese!

No—wait—it's just a green sun. Here we see the Three Faces of Bran: Dad is already going in his drawers—and lovin' it, to judge from his expression. Mom has just got the signal from the basement that a delivery is on the way, so to speak; after a week of costive inaction it's a most pleasant sensation. Daughter is dismayed and mortified at the sounds, which she had never before associated with the dinner table. Not until they accepted bran into their lives, anyway.

BANANA ALL-BRAN NUT BREAD

¼ cup shortening
½ cup sugar
1 egg (well beaten)
1 cup Kellogg's ALL-BRAN
1½ cups flour
2 teaspoons baking powder

½ teaspoon salt
½ teaspoon soda
½ cup chopped nut meats
1½ cups mashed bananas
2 tablespoons water
1 teaspoon vanilla extract

Cream shortening and sugar well. Add egg and ALL-BRAN. Sift flour with baking powder, salt, and soda. Mix nuts with flour and add alternately with mashed bananas to which the water has been added. Stir in vanilla. Pour into greased loaf tin. Let stand 30 minutes and bake in a moderate oven (375° F.) one hour. Let cool before cutting.

Yield: 1 loaf (8½ by 4½ inches).

(Illustrated on reverse side)

Hello, world! Let my jaunty step and upraised phallic cane show you just what bran can do to you! Why, my movement this morning was so cogent and spectacular I'm carrying it around in my pocket all day. Want a look?

Yield: 1 loaf.

Of *what*?

This? You're not sure if this the "before" or "after" picture, are you?

Get Off to a Distasteful Start with Appetizers

All hail the standard appetizer-presentation paradigm of the swank-food era: the relish plate! The standard ingredients of this fine dish were arrayed, each in their own compartment for maximum visual punch: The crinkle-cut carrots. The celery lance for the dieting ladies. Olives, ignored by all until someone suggested martinis. Sweet gherkins were a treat and usually the first wedge of the pie-chart to go. If there was a cheese component, it was Kraft Cracker Barrel Sharp Cheddar, with a complement of buttery Ritz crackers on the side.

This was the appetizer plate in the 1950s and 60s. This was the law; Hoover sent around a warning letter if you were to deviate from the norm. The days of jicama sticks and goat-cheese dip were many years away. But sometimes hostesses would draw the drapes and dim the lights and serve things that weren't on the official appetizer agenda. Here are some of the secret appetizers, served by the bold and the brave.

The rare Plate Crab (*Appetizerus bogus*)

The plate crab is capable of remaining motionless for hours. It uses its false eyes to mesmerize prey until the prey comes to believe the crab is actually edible; when the victim touches the center, the arms snap shut over the hapless soul's wrist. It can dissolve the flesh from a hand in thirty minutes.

So if you bring this to a potluck, don't put your name on masking tape on the bottom of the dish.

Every party,
Satan brings
the same
damn thing.

Speared Souls Bobbing in Creamed Lava, served in a Penis Pot. It was amusing the first time—everyone thought Satan was being ironic, you know, playing to type, satirizing our expectations by fulfilling them, but after a few years it was obvious that's all the dude knows how to make.

Actually, no, one year he did bring something different: He called it Hell-Souls Lanced with Torment Sticks, or something like that. It was marshmallows rolled in confetti with a cocktail onion on top. Seriously. And he was all, like, Behold! And we were like, *Hey, that's cool,* but no one touched them.

BURNING BUSH

Dried beef

½-lb. pkg. Philadelphia Brand Cream Cheese

Grapefruit, or large red apple

Chop the dried beef very fine. Divide the cream cheese into 32 cubes, then roll each cube into a ball, on butter paddles. Toss each ball in the chopped beef until entirely coated. Put a toothpick through each ball, and stick onto a grapefruit, or large apple.

And Moses spake unto the Lord, and didst ask: "Whatfore then shall I serveth those who doth arrive like a man who cometh early to the feast, but turneth away from the radish plate?"

And the Lord spoke unto Moses: "Behold, I come to thee in a pleasing array of moistureless beef and cream cheese."

And Moses was full afraid, and knelt down, asking, "Define 'pleasing,' O my Lord."

And the Lord said: "Thou shalt take a fourth part of thine hides and loins and chop them until the fineness shall be very; the cream cheese shall be formed into spheres one one-thousandth of a cubit in diameter, and on these balls shalt thou construct a skin of meat against the paddles thine women have anointed with butter. Impaleth it with the youngest of sticks and arrange it in a manner that pleaseth thine most discriminating guest. Thou shalt call it 'The Burning Bush.'"

And Moses saith, his voice full confused with wonder, "It burns not, yet it is consumed."

And the Lord said, "Pretty much, yeah."

Hello there. I'm Earl Warren. You may remember me from such unsatisfying official assessments of a presidential assassination as "The Warren Report." But I'm here today to talk about olives. They're nature's most testicular fruit. No—wait, they're not a fruit. Or are they? Doesn't seem right. They don't seem like vegetables, either. Well, I don't know why they have to be one or the other. Let's just call them olives and leave it at that.

Anyway, here we see an example of our California custom, in which olives are put in bowels. Sorry, I mean bowls. Although now that you think about it, "bowels" is right, eventually, although the "California Olive Bowel" sounds like a form of colitis common to raw-food fanatics. In any case! It's such an easy way to say "welcome"—although not as easy as forming the word with your lips and expelling breath to make the actual sound, of course.

SALTY BREADSTICKS

1 package active dry yeast
¾ cup warm water (105 to 115°)
2½ cups Bisquick
¼ cup butter or margarine, melted
Salt or garlic salt

Dissolve yeast in warm water. Mix in Bisquick; beat vigorously. Turn dough onto surface well dusted with Bisquick. Knead until smooth, about 20 times. Divide dough into 16 equal parts. Roll each piece between hands into pencil-like strip, 8 inches long. Spread part of butter in oblong pan, 13x9x2 inches. Place strips of dough in pan. Brush tops with remaining butter; sprinkle with salt. Cover and let rise in warm place (85°) until light, about 1 hour.

Heat oven to 425°. Bake breadsticks 15 minutes or until light golden brown. Turn off oven; allow breadsticks to remain in oven 15 minutes longer to crisp. *Makes 16 sticks.*

ZUCCHINI TOSS

1 head lettuce, torn into bite-size pieces
1 head romaine, torn into bite-size pieces
2 medium zucchini, thinly sliced
1 cup sliced radishes
2 tablespoons sliced green onions
3 tablespoons salad oil
Garlic Dressing (below)

Toss salad greens, zucchini, radishes and onion with salad oil just until leaves glisten. Toss with Garlic Dressing. *6 to 8 servings.*

ANISE TOAST

2 eggs
⅔ cup sugar
1 teaspoon anise seed
1 cup Gold Medal Flour (regular or Wondra)

Heat oven to 375°. Grease and flour a loaf pan, 9x5x3 inches. Beat eggs and sugar in small mixing bowl until light and fluffy. Add anise seed; gradually mix in flour. Push batter into prepared pan. Bake about 20 minutes, or until wooden pick inserted in center comes out clean. (Pan will be only ¼ full.) Remove from pan and cut loaf into ¼-inch slices. Place slices on buttered baking sheet; bake 3 to 4 minutes, or until slices are browned on bottom. Turn slices; bake 3 to 4 minutes longer, or until slices are browned on other side. *Makes 32 slices.*

FRUIT TRAY

Mix-matching fruit and cheese for dessert is such an easy, adventuresome and spectacular way to end a meal. Start with your prettiest plate or wooden platter or a tiered compote. Arrange on it a variety of cheeses, choosing those that will give you different flavors and textures. As a guide, select at least one soft, one semisoft and one hard cheese; some mild and some sharp.

If you don't get it, that's fine.

Don't ask a teenager if they get it, because they'll get all flustered trying to explain. If you do get it, and you're offended, well, I didn't say anything. In fact I'm not even starting to think about getting a flashlight and ladder to head up to the attic to find that ten-foot pole with which this will not be touched. Address all complaints c/o Unforeseen Shifts in Language Bureau, 1961 Innocent Boulevard, Anytown, USA.

In retrospect, it was obvious that three straight nights of making pie charts for the sales presentation had affected Mommy more than anyone suspected.

Pizza was still a novelty in the fifties.

It was viewed with a certain amount of suspicion. After all, it was an ethnic food favored by colorful, swarthy ethnic types who had handlebar mustaches and *"spoke-a like-a this-a, eh? Mamma mia!"* Pizza had to be domesticated, in other words, and since you couldn't make it sign a Loyalty Oath, that meant stepping down the flavor. This was the final result: a quarter-inch-thick pie crust that tasted like saltine crackers, a gentle smear of ketchup, and a pound of salty cheese. For toppings? Ninja-throwing-star anchovies.

En route to the farm, Mom consoled her daughter. _"Don't be so pouty, child. Grandma always has pie and cake, doesn't she?"_

"She has fish pie, Mom! It's PIE WITH FISH. And I don't know what that cake is. It's like creamed _mice_, or something. And even her water tastes weird. It's like she washes the glasses with her nylons. "

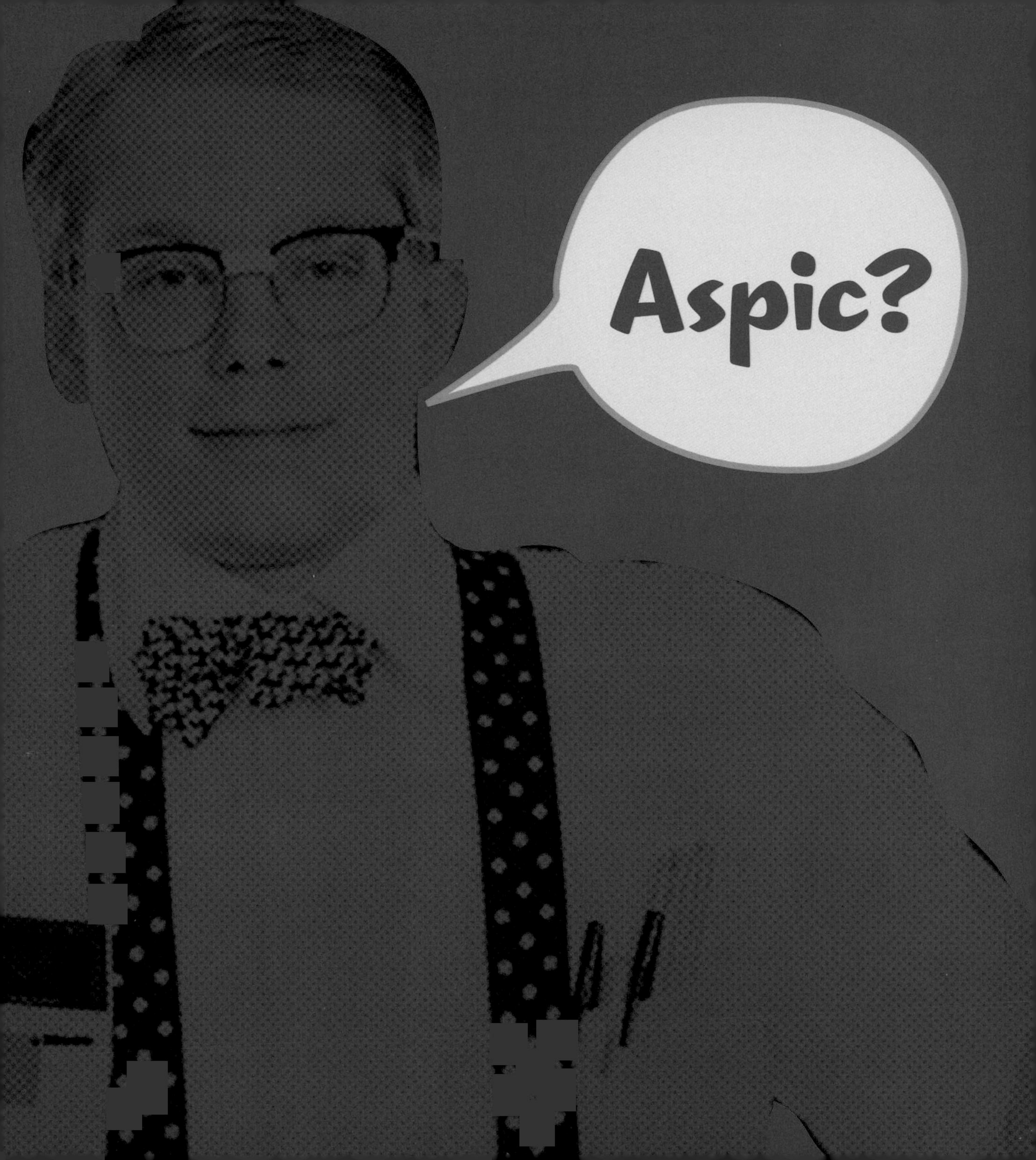
Aspic?

The Wonderful World of Aspics

Aspic? What's an aspic? Ask any uncouth youth at the mall, and they'd probably say it's a device for reorienting thong underwear. But once upon a time, the aspic was a staple of the American dinner–a cold, wobbly, trembling thing that entombed hapless food in its gelatinous grip.

Herewith is a sample of the aspics American women were permitted–nay, encouraged–to foist on friends and relations.

This is an aspic.

It hails from a book called *Diet Delights,* although it could also be a plate from an encyclopedia of diseases that affect the internal organs of circus clowns.

Grass aspic? Grasspic? Whatever: It only takes a few hours to chill, but you spend the whole damn afternoon shoving the lawn-mower clippings into the blender. For extra gag-ability, make sure the potatoes are full of lumps, because there's nothing like Grass Aspic with Tater Cysts to make the young folk at the table throw up in their napkins. Don't forget the Boiled Eggs à la Firing Squad, either.

SLICED CHICKEN AND VEGETABLES IN ASPIC

Aww, how sweet.

Three little slices of meat, all tucked in for the night.

Just for fun, kids: Find the chicken! Is it in the cold foundation stratum loaded with boiled carrots like unexploded depth charges? No. Is it in the middle layer, which looks like a close-up view of a virus-laden bloodstream? No. Is the chicken in the top layer? Perhaps—if broth form counts.

So where's the chicken? Down the street at the place with the friendly old Southern colonel on the sign, which is where you wish you were right now.

Put your ear close.

If you listen, you can actually hear the meat *screaming in terror*.

The caption tells us the composition of the upper story: corned beef and beef-flavored gelatin. We may lament the absence of cow Jell-O from the modern table, but let this not blind us from the curious foundation on which the Beef à la Jiggly rests. Some sort of industrial gear coated with fire-retardant foam, perhaps.

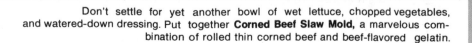

Don't settle for yet another bowl of wet lettuce, chopped vegetables, and watered-down dressing. Put together **Corned Beef Slaw Mold,** a marvelous combination of rolled thin corned beef and beef-flavored gelatin.

Bivalve Chunky Spackle Fungus!

Well, three out of four ain't bad. Your guests may wonder: How *did* you make the mushrooms float above the chicken-liver treat-slab? Superconducting magnets, as used by French and Japanese high-speed transit lines? Did you charge the mushrooms with negative-ion particles and use the fluctuating polarity to fix them in stasis? Your guests are *nerds*.

CHICKEN LIVER-MUSHROOM TREAT

Top right: Chicken Curry Salad. The recipe says "toss lightly," but that depends on how much you eat and how bad the cramps get. The item at the top left is a cross-section of the Holiday Salad, although which holiday is best celebrated with Tumor-Studded Bruise Cake is not entirely certain. On the bottom: Corned Beef Salad Loaf Aspic, which is meat in its most dog-confusing form. Their nose tells them it's meat, but it's meat that's gone horribly awry.

How to Drive Off Your Husband with Lousy Cooking

How many wives were disappointed to discover *51 Ways to a Man's Heart* wasn't a book about poison?

He seems to be in pain, after all—either the first twinge of belladonna has just paralyzed his left ventricle, or someone emptied a turkey-baster full of lemon juice in his eye. No matter: Hubby's going *down*. If your goal is getting rid of that self-satisfied sack of flab you face every morning in the breakfast nook, the recipes that follow can accomplish the goal quite nicely.

Not as quickly as poison, but the coppers look for those things nowadays.

51 Ways
to a Man's Heart
BY ANNA LEE SCOTT

Step one: Roadkill à la tomate.

Find a fish on the shore, preferably one whose tail has been pre-consumed by various predators; remove head (if present) and stuff with those white clover things your daughter collects because she thinks they're flowers. Use bacon to simulate a tire tread. Garnish with whatever meaningless edibles you have around the kitchen—what matters is that they are symmetrically arranged, because later tonight you will order the items on his nightstand so they're all pointed in the same direction. Then you will sort his coins on the bureau by denomination, as well as the bills in his wallet. Eventually your silent insistence on total order will make him crack, and stay out late after work in a bar shooting hot lusty looks at a cheap dame who throws the peanut shells on the floor and doesn't give a damn how they land. She'll leave something on his collar—lipstick, a drugstore knockoff of Tabu. That's when you'll go to the lawyers.

If that doesn't work, proceed to the next step.

Roast pigeons are not too luxurious when two are enough for the family

Step two:
Meet him in the park for lunch.

Carry a net and some seed; turn away his inquiries with a coquettish smile, and tell him he'll see soon enough, silly. (Tap the tip of his nose with your index finger as you say this.)

Serve this for supper. When he asks what the hell this is, because it tastes like a chicken that drowned in a septic tank, calmly repeat the menu book's assertion. Roast pigeons are not too luxurious when two are enough for the family. He won't know what it means. No one does.

If this didn't drive him off, proceed to step three.

Step three: Play with his mind.

If he's an *Aliens* movie fan serve this. Attach thin filaments such as sewing thread or dental floss to the extremities; loop over light fixture; tie ends to a piece of dead mouse and leave it under the table. When the cat plays with the mouse, the limbs will jerk, causing immediate cardiac arrest in your husband. Remove filaments; call police.
If this fails, proceed to step four.

SOUP FROM CHICKEN FEET

Singe chicken feet, wash well, drop into scalding water and let stand 10 minutes. Skin; cover with cold water in a kettle; season and cook until they fall apart.

Step four: Pull out the stops.

Tell him dinner will be late, because the skinned, singed chicken feet haven't fallen apart yet. Then serve him tea with mushrooms and toothpicks, and pretend like everything's normal.

He's still around? Can't let you go? He's madly, desperately, hopelessly in love with you? Maybe you can turn this to your advantage. Have affairs all over town, and throw them in his face. Make chicken feet soup, and throw *that* in his face. Sneer about his paltry paycheck, and ask why he can't stand up to the boss—and when he comes home with a wheedling smile on his pathetic face, well, you know what to do: Proceed to step five.

Step five: Ruin his career.

As we all know, there's no more terrifying event in a man's professional life than the night the boss comes over for dinner. One wrong move and Hubby can forget about that promotion. When he's passed over again for a managerial job, and screws up the nerve to ask why, the boss will spell it out, cold and curt: *The pork had a hint of pink. Can't trust a man who can't keep his house in order, Johnson.* Why the old bastard feels the need to have supper with his quaking slaves, you can only guess; probably married to some thick-ankled battle-axe who keeps a bottle of gin in the hothouse, gets sloshed by five and works dinner conversation around to affairs she's certain he has with the girls in the secretarial pool. And that wounds him, it really does; even if they'd have him, it would be a joyless thing, a cruel demonstration of the prerogatives of power. It happened once, years ago, and the poor girl cried afterwards. *Cried.*

Anyway, when the boss comes over, serve him this. Run your tongue along your lips and ask the boss if he ever planked a lamb. Laugh at inappropriate times. Make everyone feel uncomfortable. Call his wife later and offer to send over the recipe.

Help your husband get his raise by serving the boss planked lamb chops with a border of mashed potatoes

42

Unexpected guests will not daunt a hostess who knows how to make a Fish Roll

And if she can make it sit up and beg, all the better.

The ingredients for the bottom item can be found at any art supply store. Oil-based paints are best.

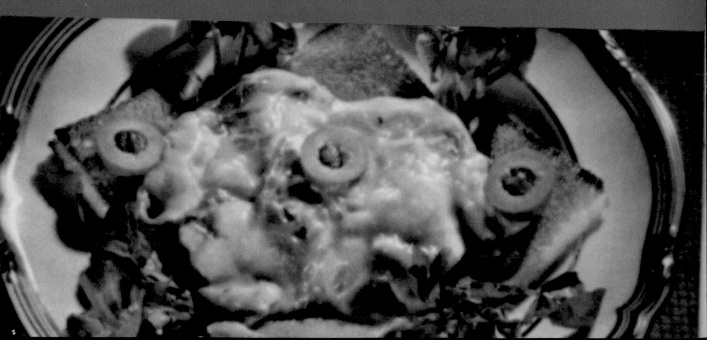

This is not a meal.
This is a Ripley's Believe It Or Not photo of conjoined bovines, joined at the head.

BEEF COOKERY

The night has a thousand eyes. And so does the main course.

And now it's time for dessert!

Here we see a common problem with black-and-white food photos. Ice cream—or *meat?*

Of course, there's no reason it couldn't be both. At this point the boss no longer feels pity for your husband; he feels only contempt. Congratulations! You've started your husband down the road to chronic drinking, which will make it easier to arrange that "accident" a few months down the line. But be patient. Tonight you cry. After the boss leaves and your husband turns on you with a furious face—What the hell *was* that? Was that even *food?*—you cry. You apologize. You fix him a drink. A nice stiff drink. Get him loaded, sister, because the coup de grace comes tomorrow when he wakes with a clanging hangover in time for lunch.

This will make him pack his bags.

Taunt him as he leaves. "Some folks throw away that old asbestos insulation after they take it off the pipes," you shrug. "Some folks must just be *made* of money."

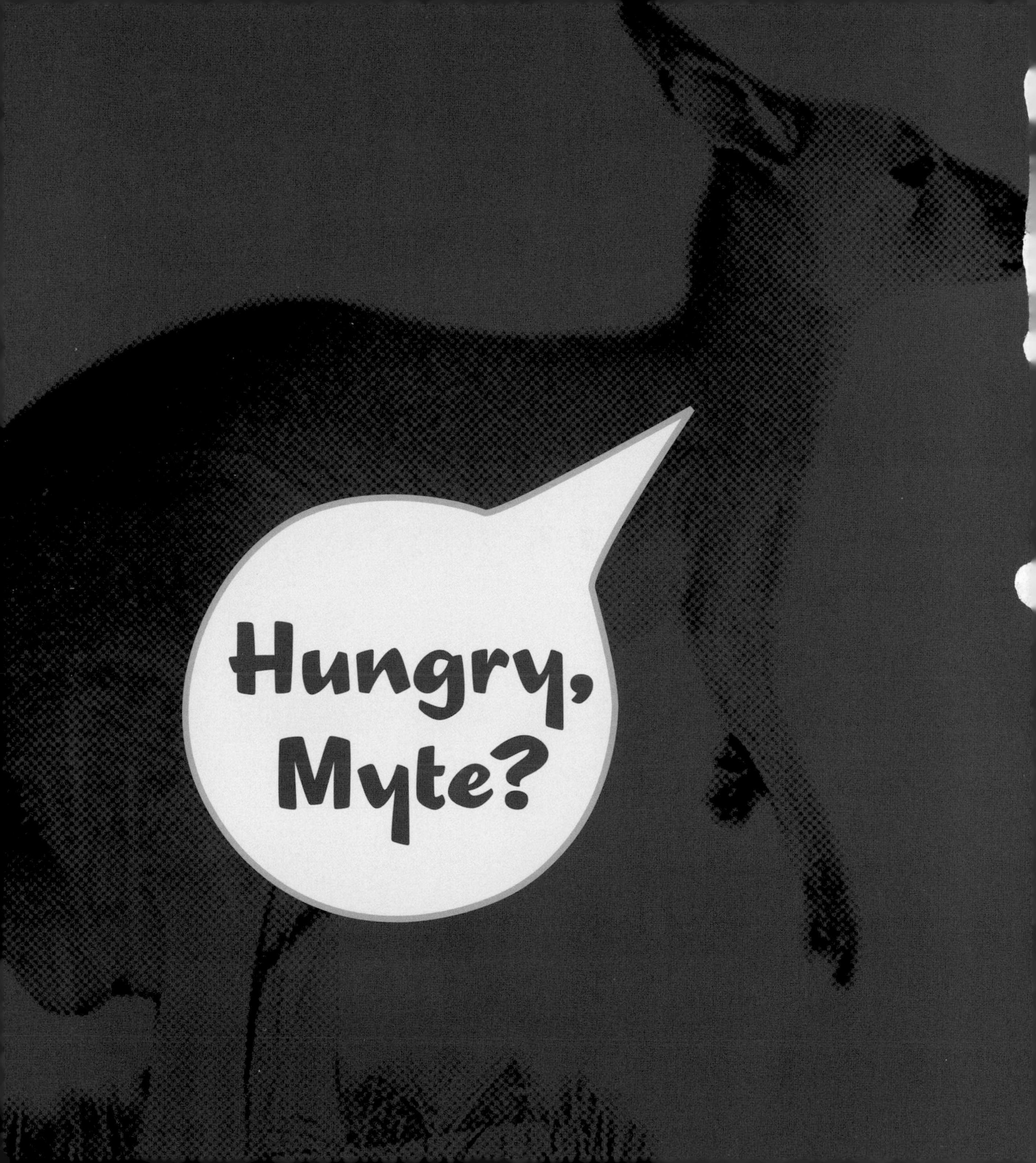
Hungry, Myte?

Chunder from
Down Under

Ah, the Australians: cheeky, fun-loving, brave, stalwart allies. And judging from this early fifties cookbook, a country that didn't even try to have a national cuisine. Food, it seems, was a grim necessity, nothing more; like sex to the Victorians, it was something to be gotten over quickly with a minimum of pleasure and enthusiasm. Let's take a brief tour of Antipodean edibles, and be warned: No expense was spared in making these dishes look as unpalatable as possible.

THE AUSTRALIAN WOMEN'S WEEKLY
COOKERY
IN COLOUR
edited by
LEILA HOWARD
AND
MARGUERITE PATTEN

Australia's early history as a penal colony,

with an unnatural ratio of men to women, produced a lamentable genre of sexually aggressive sandwich-making styles.

The inventor of this particular treat insisted for years that the bread had asked for it.

Scales 'n' bones 'n' blood 'n' butter!
Beulah couldn't *wait* to try out her new Kitchen Guillotine.

People today expect their fish to be a bit more . . . disguised. This looks like something you found on the floor after the cat got into the aquarium.

By now you should realize

the importance of bread in Australian snacks. Bread into which things have been poked, and bread onto which things have been placed. Now you must begin to confront the importance of bacon. (Pronounced "baiycun"!)

The above photo is a simple and inoffensive example, but if you need a cookbook to tell you to make this, it's a hint you're not talking about the French. Note the absence of a toothpick, which suggests that the rolled-up wads of baiycun are held in place by melted glue-based cheese. It's probably delicious, but it looks like something a fourth-grader would invent. Anyway, it's burned. That's not baiycun.

The photo to the right? *This* is baiycun.

This, too, is baiycun.

It was apparently taken from pigs that were beaten to death; hence the bruised color. Serve with fresh canned semicircles (if in season) and skinned pan-blacked monkey fingers on the side.

And more baiycun yet!

Or pan-boiled albino slug-husks; rather hard to tell. The waffles seem properly horrified by the stuff, though. *Get it off me! Augh!* **Get it off!**

Then again, sometimes a chap likes his baiycun in handy slab form:

224 CASSEROLE OF BACON

Choose one of the cuts of bacon suggested in the table, Recipe No. 163. Soak for some hours or overnight in cold water. Put into a casserole with various vegetables and water, or use cider for an excellent flavour. Cover the casserole with foil or a lid and cook gently allowing 20—25 minutes per lb. in a moderately hot oven or about 35—40 minutes per lb. in a very moderate oven. Apples, prunes, raisins are some of the more unusual ingredients that can be put into the casserole, as well as vegetables — or instead of them.

Do not thicken the liquid before cooking, but season well with mustard.

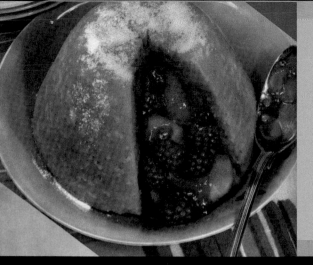

If this was a person, and this was exploratory surgery, they'd just sew him back up and tell him to get his affairs in order.

Try the new sensation, Rash-Burgers! Melted squares of beige vinyl raincoat top this delicious mixture of bread, cheese, and marinated serving-cart wheels.

The impact of nearby Asian cultures

on Australian cuisine cannot be underestimated, or excused.

The arrangement of these Chinese Stuffed Cucumbers actually forms a Mandarin character that means "irritable bowel syndrome."

Well crikey, myte! Just because the horse died
in a fire doesn't mean the bones can't be used for stock.

Now, where's my *baiycun?*

Sometimes, just for fun, leave the head on! There's nothing like blank dead eyes and an exploded lower jaw to add a gay note to a party. Don't forget the pimientos—arrange them like radio knobs, and watch your drunken guests desperately try to tune in a different meal.

On the left, Cirrhosis Souffle, a mainstay

of the local diet. The item on the right is a dingo haunch, also known as
Convict Cutlet, and was given to men with long prison terms; it took an entire
day to chew, and thus helped to pass the time.

633   **TOAD-IN-THE-HOLE**

¾—1 lb. sausages or   *Yorkshire pudding batter*
    meat mixture*   *(Recipe No. 636)*
                                 knob fat or dripping if
                                 required

* Instead of sausages you can use canned frankfurter sausages,
kidneys, tomatoes, fingers of steak or a selection of these

When the recipe allows you to substitute

something with "meat mixture,"
you know the dish will not be
presented to visiting royalty. Or
maybe it will, just to remind the
Crown that we don't stand on
ceremony in these parts, and if
you're a good Sheila with fair
dinkum on 'er you'll tuck in.

'Ere, Your Majesty—some more knob fat?

Some of them things we got off a bush,

and some of them we got off the sheep.

Now, most of these we got off the sheep, but some of them we got off Nigel's neck.

What's that?

You want something lighter? Fair enough, myte:

We call this the Poofter Detector. I'm not saying we wonder about the guys who take one, myte, but we might wonder about the blokes what take one straightaway.

Crikey!

You beat me again! Have you been practicin', now?

Fun Things to Make with Ground-Up Cow

Everyone likes hamburgers. Even vegetarians. If they say they don't want a hamburger they are *lying*. This is how some attorneys used to get them tossed off juries, incidentally, which is why they can't ask people if they're vegans anymore. Pity: People who say they do not like hamburgers cannot be trusted. If they can lie about that, well, they can lie about anything. Because *everyone likes hamburgers*. No one who swears off vegetables ever wakes in the night crying out for celery, but someone who turned his back on meat forty years ago still sees the burgers of his youth in his dreams. Not the flat banal fast-food divots, but inch-thick char-kissed pucks slathered with cheddar goo, savory ketchup, piquant mustard, bacony bacon, and crisp sinus-tweaking onions, all crowned by a butter-kissed toasted bun. *Ahhh.*

Behold the Elephant Man Burger.

I am not a bacon-topped tower of inexpertly piled foodstuffs! I am a human being!

A spinoff of the Space Program, the Multi-Stage Burger used the lower portion to loft the meal into the stratosphere, after which the onion-based inter-stage seal would disengage, allowing the upper meat capsule to attain orbital position.

Two cups of sour cream were always standing by, in case there was a fire on the launching pad.

The vegan version of a Roman crucifixion, or a Cambodian temple re-created with ground chuck and mushrooms? It all depends on the theme of your party.

Char-seared tricycle tire

with a pilaf of rice, studded with black lightbulbs.

69

An onion ring is not a bun.

*An onion ring is **not** a bun,* the man insists. It is an adjunct to the bun, yea; it complements the yielding flesh of the topmost bread with its piquant salty crust, but it cannot stand in the stead of bread itself. The man must *clutch* something to bear the treasure to the waiting mouth. A bottom bun must have its mate. It is the way of things, the yin and the yang, the hat to the spats, the—

Hold on, what the hell—is that the top bun on the left? Smothered with *$#$% creamed beans? Do you *honestly* expect two thin onion rings to prevail under these conditions? Is this some kind of sick *joke?*

We're not suggesting the middle layer looks like topsoil, but if you stuck a venus flytrap seed in that loamy meat, it would probably grow four feet tall and have the power to snatch parakeets from the air in midflight.

If your family tires of Sloppy Joes, consider dry, celery-infested chopped turkey served on a deflated breast implant, garnished with stage blood.

The middle devil-cow skewer says

"Medium Rare." Look, pal: It's impossible to make medium-rare sloppy joes, unless you mix in raw beef with the cooked stuff, in which case you might as well administer *E. coli* via nasal swabs to all your houseguests. The square burgers look tasty, but don't forget to pierce them with useless vegetables skewered by a rectal thermometer. Place sandwiches near 45 rpm records to indicate that they are "keen" and "gear" and otherwise attractive to teenagers; deploy a "mod" tablecloth to show that you are "with it" and "relevant." Be prepared to squander all that transient credibility the second you find one of the boys in the backyard with his hand up your daughter's blouse, because you're going to say things about him and Vietnam and what he should be doing instead of pretending he's the second coming of Andy gosh-darn Warhol, mister.

Honestly, the *nerve.* The *cheek.*

Delicious Fast Forward Burgers

remind teens of the button they love to push when things get boring. But there's nothing boring about these burgers! The "kiss o' heat" cooking technique ensures that maximum slaughterhouse contamination will find its way to your table.

Even the sauce seems to be making a desperate break for it.

Domestic napalm
in handy sprayable form.

Pity Siz didn't last; there are few things manlier than cooking ground beef with explosive shaving cream. You suspect that Billy and Bobby snuck a can of Siz out of Dad's shed and laid a line down the sidewalk, with firecrackers and green plastic Army men embedded in the combustible trail. One of the soldiers actually shot through the garage wall. Wicked!

REVOLUTIONARY CHARCOAL LIGHTER FOR THE COOKOUT CHAMPIONSHIP...

NEW BAR-B-TRICK

New "SIZ" makes cooking coals in half the time

Charcoal lights instantly with this amazing sizzling action foam. Just apply "SIZ" once, with finger-tip pressure. Then, toss in one match. "SIZ" does the rest. Holds each coal in a clutch of fire. "SIZ" burns at more than 1120° Fahrenheit—hotter than any other charcoal lighter. "SIZ" burns longer, too. Turns your charcoal bed into even-burning cooking coals twice as fast as ordinary lighters.

No false starts: You apply just once, light just once. No lighter run-off: "SIZ" clings to each briquet. No soaking necessary. Finger-tip control ends lighter waste. "SIZ" is your best value in the charcoal lighter field today. (Will not affect food flavor.) Look for revolutionary new "SIZ" wherever charcoal is sold or displayed.

FROM THE MAKERS OF "GLASS WAX." "SIZ," "GLASS WAX" AND "GOLD SEAL" are trademarks of the Gold Seal Co., Bismark, N. Dak.

GET INSTANT "SIZ" CHARCOAL LIGHTER—TWICE AS FAST AS ORDINARY LIGHTERS

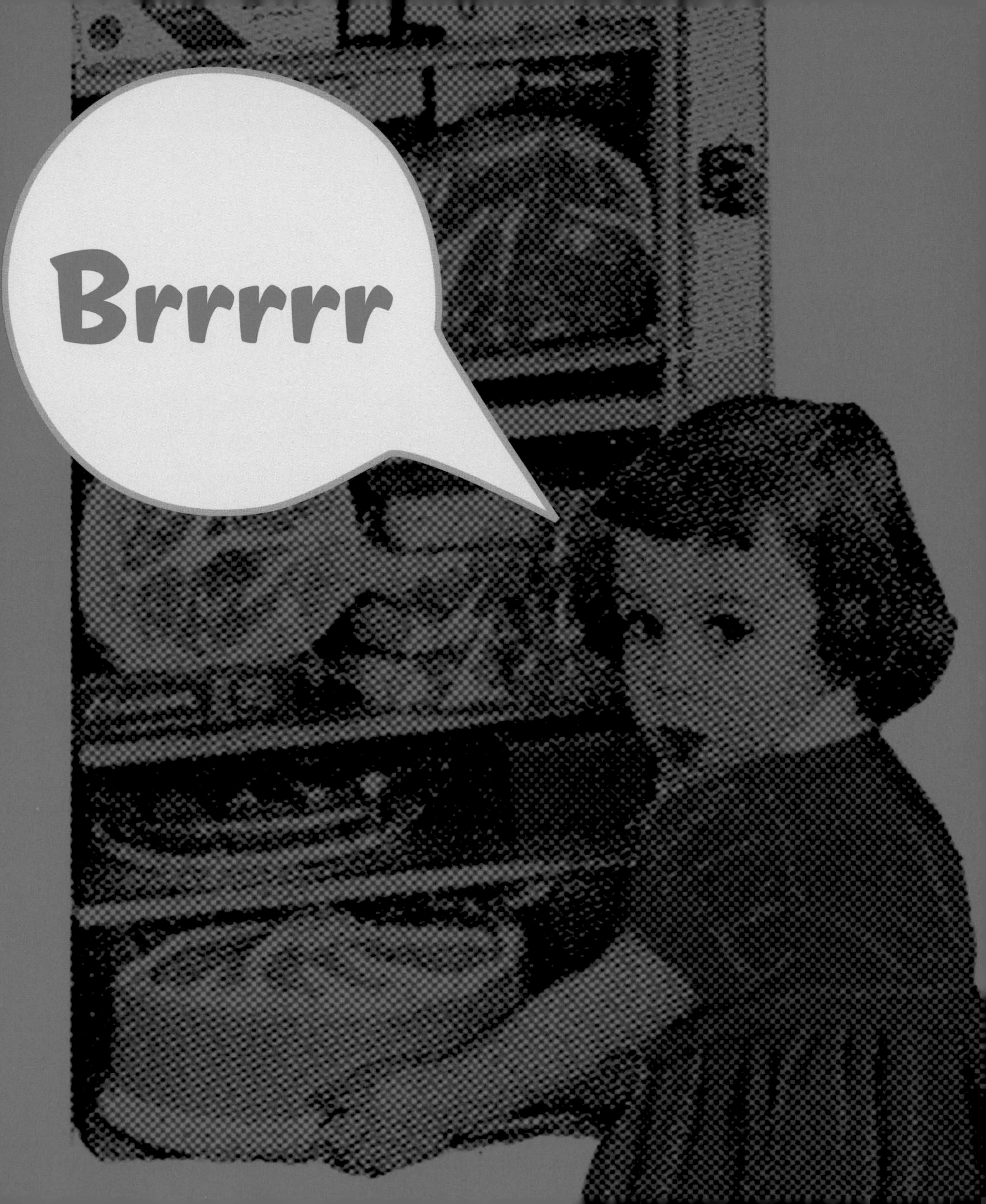
Brrrrr

All Hail the Miraculous Magic Cold Box

At this point a brief time-out is required; one can only look at so many examples of gut-unnerving meals without pausing to fortify the nerves. Let's take a look at the marvelous Freon-filled machines in which these meals were stored.

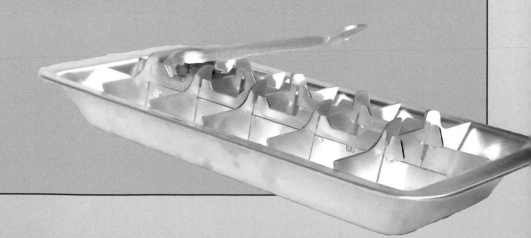

The original. The Model T of fridges.

It weighed seventeen tons, had a spinning blade on top with a grill wide enough for curious little fingers, and had a wee snowy freezer compartment that resembled a scene from the Abominable Snowman's colonoscopy. It didn't have a lighted interior, unless you painted the interior with phosphorescent radium. In which case your grave would still set off a Geiger counter fifty years after you were buried.

In the prewar era, a woman had to get down on her stomach and crawl like a reptile to get things from the bottom shelf—but that was before Crosley bestowed the Shelvador upon the world. *You need never bend over again.* Note how the demonstrator seems to be a single woman—apron free, jaunty and confident, bringing the boon of door shelves to the Wife-American community. The other woman, whose marital status is signified by a sheath over her birthin' parts, is caught in a strange and delirious rapture—her hand smooths the face of the breadwinner who has agreed to go into debt for this unit, and as a reward for his largesse he's allowed to touch her in a fashion that would pass the network censors.

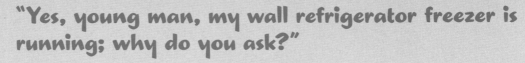

"Yes, young man, my wall refrigerator freezer is running; why do you ask?"

Pity this refrigerator didn't catch on; it's pretty nifty. Possible reasons for failure:

1. When it fell, it took most of the wall with it, along with all of the wife.
2. Patented "NevR Cloz" doors led to spoilage.
3. Had the storage capacity of a largish glove compartment.
4. Was part of a promised future that also involved flying cars, motorized walkways and atomic piles in the basement, and we know how that turned out.
5. Never built; was leaked to the press just to make Russian engineers waste time developing their own versions.
6. It just felt wrong, that's all. Fridges are vertical free-standing devices with big doors. (See facing page, for example.)

This is a fridge.

This is a gorgeous mid-fifties Kelvinator, and the only thing it's missing is tailfins. It's also about twelve inches deep, which means you could probably pull it over trying to get one of those ice trays out of the freezer.

You know: these. Metal trays that adhered to the freezer floor, could not be handled with slightly wet hands without significant loss of epidermis, shattered 90 percent of the ice cubes upon usage, and accumulated glacier-dense layers of undead ice in the corners that required immersion in hot water to clean. Then you'd put it back in the freezer. Then you'd remember: that's what made it stick.

On the other hand, it's pink!

If there's a branch of feng shui that involves the maximum arrangement of meat in a confined space, we know who's perfected it.

GE! They bring good things to life, and keep the dead things from going bad. But the real appeal of this '57 classic was the "Book-Shelf" concept: assuming all your frozen foods came in boxes of identical sizes, you could arrange them like those Reader's Digest Condensed Books you never read. Which no doubt inflamed the sensibilities of the neighborhood Germaine Greer, who sneered at the ad: *Dense bricks of cryogenically processed peas are not books! It's a transparent attempt to give the slavery of domesticity a sham veneer of erudition, as if selecting a cold box of Birds-eye was the same thing as pulling a copy of* The Collected Poems of Sappho *from a shelf! Can't you see?*

Yes, I suppose, but it's so neat. And it's pink!

New General Electric "Book-Shelf" Freezer

puts <u>twice</u> as much food within easy reach as a chest freezer!

No "standing on your head" rummaging for food.

Your food is easy to reach... like taking books off a shelf.

Yes, this new General Electric "Book-Shelf" Freezer keeps 640 pounds of frozen foods as easy to reach as books on a shelf.

Beats chests and other uprights on exterior design, too. You can put this new General Electric Freezer right up against your kitchen cabinets... or fit it flush with a corner wall... gives a "built-in" look without remodeling expense.

And, you get a 20-juice-can dispenser, 2-gallon ice cream conditioner, sliding basket for bulky items, plus a choice of right- or left-hand door.

Priced low, too! See the outstanding General Electric "Book-Shelf" Freezers at your local G-E dealer's now and compare with chest freezers of comparable quality and size.

Household Refrigerator Department, General Electric Company, Appliance Park, Louisville 1, Kentucky.

Progress Is Our Most Important Product

GENERAL ⓖⒺ ELECTRIC

Choice of 18- or 13-cubic-foot capacity in General Electric Mix-or-Match colors: Canary Yellow, Turquoise Green, Petal Pink, Woodtone Brown and White.

18-cubic-foot "Book-Shelf" FREEZER

83

New Space Age Magna-Hold

pulls cans from the back of the freezer, and latches on to your jewelry to keep you from leaving the kitchen and getting a job in an office where life plays out in a rich, cosmopolitan environment so different from the bright empty cage you call "home."

Unit can be used to conceal false door to cellar in case things get bad again and you have to hide your Jewish neighbors.

Each shelf is capable of supporting a single-digit number.

Now, Frigidaire sells Sheer Look colors at the Price of White!

MAKE YOUR OLD KITCHEN LOOK NEW WITHOUT REMODELING

SHEER LOOK GOWNS *by* SANDOVAL

The priestesses *had convened to invoke* Perpendiculus, the ancient god of intersecting lines. The one on the left was seven feet tall, it seemed, and you knew that if their arms came down, you would see they had no mouths. That's when you woke screaming.

But once you'd calmed down, wiped the sweat from your brow, and turned the pillow around, you realized you wanted a new fridge. Why? Simple. This picture was part of a campaign to convince Americans to upgrade their appliances. Why? Because the old ones had rounded corners, and round was out. Hard angles were in, and we've been living with the consequence ever since. Fridges and freezers have been boxy for fifty years—and just like tailfins and skinny ties, round-corned appliances are something they'll never let us have again.

END ICE TRAY TROUBLE! No more spilling! New ice tray filler* works with turn of a dial *inside* freezer; shuts itself off. New ice ejector zips out cubes, stores ice in convenient server bin!

Gentlemen!

If we can put a man in orbit and safely return him to Earth, why can't we develop an ice-making system that compensates for middle-aged men's inner-ear disorder? Not a day goes by without a complaint from the field: My husband has a poor sense of balance, and cannot put the ice trays in the freezer without spilling water down the front of his trousers! Let us get our finest minds on this.

It looks like a grand idea, but you know everyone ended up using a screwdriver to loosen the frozen trays.

CUT FOOD SPOILAGE! New Air Purifying System forces air through ultraviolet rays (1); retards growth of air-borne mold and bacteria! Cold, clean air recirculates (2) up the door (3).

UV rays help give your meat a healthy, youthful tan!

Ah, but what if you had a boring old white fridge,

and you hated it *hated it* **hated** *it?* Simple: consult the headless anthropomorphic can-man who sprays lung-paving baby-pink paint out his esophagus:

Nowadays, if a man came home and found his wife spray-painting the fridge, he would assume she had lost her mind. "There was a can with legs, John ! I saw it! It told me to make everything Baby Pink! I *do* so want a baby, John—tell me you do! Tell me you do!"

"Marion, you know what the doctor said."

"THE DOCTOR NEVER MET THE CAN WITH LEGS!"

"Lie down, Marion. Come one. Some rest, that'll set you right."

Later he opens the fridge, and finds everything has been Krylonized glossy black. His *beer* is black. On the other hand, the paint is dry to the touch. Whatever. Hell of a day, and as long as it's cold, that's what matters.

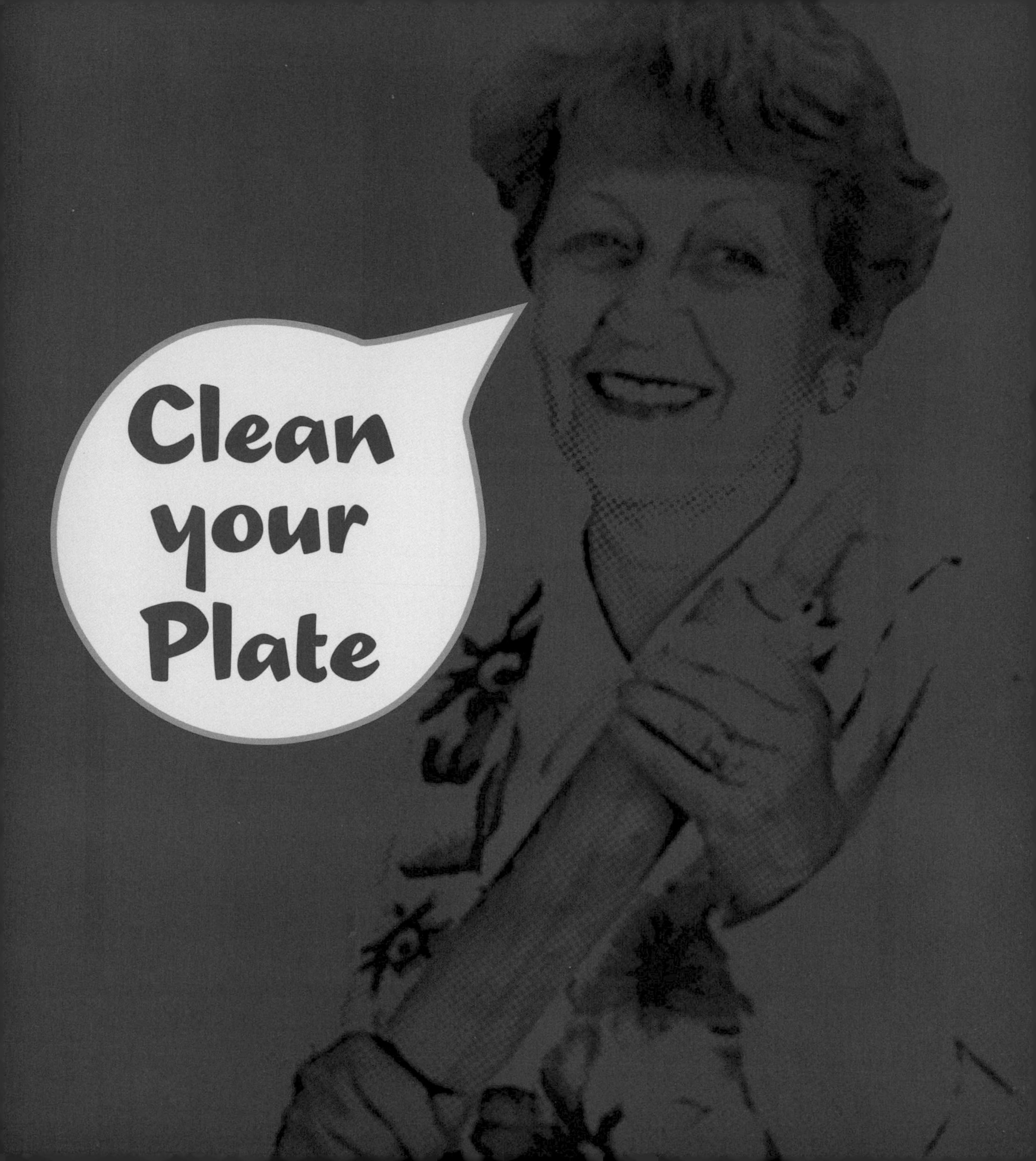
Clean your Plate

Meals Like Grandma Used to Make. Sadly

Some dishes are intriguing: they beguile with their strange allure, their audacious bravado, their modified nouns, et cetera. Other dishes manage to stick a knuckle in your gut the moment they're set on the table. Usually it's grandma food. You go over to the nice old lady's house, drink the weak coffee, eat a dusty circus peanut, chat about Things Today and how they're Strange and Annoying. And then comes the meal, which looks like vomit from the Creature from the Black Lagoon.

May we present: Grandma's source material.

Everyone likes a casserole, especially one that appears already half-digested for your convenience. This one you can make with the garbage disposal! Simply poke a variety of substances down the drain with a plunger handle, add that hard wild rice that always jabs the gums (substitute tiny nails, if you wish), and blend for fifteen seconds. Using a wrench, undo drain pipe from disposal; transfer contents to bucket. Serve cold or hot; doesn't matter, since no one's going near this thing, because it looks like the secret ingredient is hair.

The "gang" will love your Cholesterol Accordion!

It's crustless bread slathered in mayo and butter, with circular divots of processed meat of indeterminate origin. No one will dare touch it. Hell, *look* at it long enough and your arteries silt up.

Fresh from the kitchen
of Salvador Dalí,

it's l'Entrée Absurd! Its looks like food, yet it is obviously not.

Everyone will be asking Grandma the same question: How much time did you spend arranging those grub worms?

Farci saintongeais

It sounds like something no one hears about until they get the bad news from the doctor. *"I think I've found the reason for your gas, and I'm afraid it's Farci saintongeais."* You go home and Google *Farci saintongeais* in the hopes of finding a support group online. You mention it to someone at work, and she had an uncle who had *Farci saintongeais. "We called it a farcinoma. It was disgusting and he gave it to everyone."* So it's contagious? My God! I'll have to go live in a farci colony!

Hmm.

Bob was just released from jail after a high-speed chase that ended when the cops threw tire spikes on the road. What *shall* we make to welcome him home?

Indoor picnic on a raft—Broiler Bean-er Wiener

One sandwich serves the whole family! Makings are all old favorites—zipped-up baked beans, cheese, and franks broil till bubbly hot. Mustard and pickles top it off! Pass potato chips, relishes, cold milk. Then—big chocolate sundaes.

𝓗ere we have the 𝓑roiler 𝓑ean-er 𝓦iener, which theoretically could extend in either direction for miles. It could circumnavigate the globe and form one continuous band, for that matter. You would be driven mad constructing such a thing, of course, and they would find you hunched in a corner, reciting the directions: "pickle-frank-pickle-frank-pickle-frank MY GOD IT NEVER ENDS."

No matter how big you make it, it's going to fall apart the moment someone cuts it. You might as well serve it by dumping the beans in someone's lap, since that's how it will end up.

Turkish Toilet Tic-Tac-Toe

was only one of the rejected names for this dish.

I don't know what them aliens wanted,

but after we shot 'em, Paw, we skinned 'em an' their hands cooked up all purty-like.

When presented with a plate of organic marital aids and a tower of layered mashed yams, people's gratitude for the appearance of the bread basket is *immeasurable*.

Well, this makes sense—every foil-sealed chunk roast

needs to be baptized with a candy-corn broth, preferably by a giant hand showing us five of its many, many fingers. But what's that thing on top of the meat? A cornbread remora?

The parsley has gathered in full force in the background, ready for action in case the few flecks already deployed prove insufficient to the task. Unlikely as that may be.

Seafood seems a safe guess.

But so does cat-sick on the half-shell. Whatever it is, Granny bloodied her knuckles grating a pound of bacon.

Don't forget the parsley!

Finally!

Something that makes perfect sense. On the top right, some delightfully crispy deep-fried CDs; then some top-heavy ice cream cones that will all end up on the carpet when you try to carry the tray into the living room, leading to shrieks and weeping and hard words from the hostess about how much Old Granddad you've had tonight, Bob, and for *once* it would be nice if you'd wait until *after* dessert to get stinking drunk (tears, running from room, slammed door, uncomfortable shifting in seat by guests).

In the middle of the photo, everyone's favorite dessert: brine-soaked parsley-sanctified pole-poked pickles on ice. And you know where you can put those, Bob, don't you?

Please, Mary. Don't start.

How many "My Little Ponies"

gave their blood
for that meatball
sauce?

As Churchill said about the Soviet Union: It's a riddle wrapped within a mystery wrapped in an enigma. But this riddle is studded with ALL KINDS OF WEIRD CRAP. And hidden in a cave of bread.

Grandma, you've outdone yourself!

These truly are mystery dishes.

Taken out of the context of a recipe book, you simply cannot tell what they are by looking at them. And you don't really want to look at them at all.

Breakfast sausages + mystery chunks tossed in furniture polish = dinner? Apparently. The parsley looks like they cremated the Hulk and scattered his ashes.

Mirror, mirror, on the wall,

who's the barfiest dish of all? It's another inscrutable pan-o-heave on top of some Martian flatworms. Even the decorative cherub on the mirror is disgusted by this thing, and that takes some doing. The little guy's seen a lot.

It took years of practice,

but eventually the Zen master could stand the pot on one leg. Now Granny can do it, too.

It's not often you want your entrée to resemble aerial photographs of a mass grave, but should the need arise, here's your dish.

Takes a year to cook,

but there's nothing like Sunrise-Baked Hog-Thigh. Bring a gun, though; the couple that set up this nice picnic were abducted and buried in the desert about six weeks ago.

Horsey Road-Apple Heap, Fiesta Style! This would
make sense if the recipe book was called *Rice Cookery Secrets with Elmer's Glue*, but it's not.
How the rice maintains structural integrity is a bit of a mystery, since the entire thing is
guaranteed to fall apart the moment a fork grazes the rice.

"I broke it!" says the kid. *"Sorry, Mom!"*

"That's okay," says Mom with a wise smile. "What have we learned here?"

"Slightly dry rice fails to maintain specific shapes when breached?"

"No, dear child. Nothing beautiful lasts forever."

"Right, but if the rice had been moister—"

"I *said*, 'Nothing beautiful lasts forever.'"

"Okay, I guess."

It's not often the recipe advises you to bury the ham, which sounds like a fraternity simile for a good time. But this does look like buried skin-on pig-wad, and it looks as if it fights the tooth like a thick damp magazine.

The pimientos add dash, which is what most hardworking men want for supper at the end of a long day driving a truck or lifting greasy barrels. *Dash*.

Scalloped Ham 'n Potatoes—a hearty, one-dish-meal favorite

Ham cooks with potato slices in creamy mushroom soup. Bits of pimiento and green peppe add dash, color. Bury ham in potatoes to bake, then lift to top for serving. Keeps meat mois

Doctor, the patient is prepped and ready for surgery.

If this food was any whiter, it would be wearing pointy hats and burning crosses on the lawns of recipes for black-eyed peas. What's the secret ingredient? Bleach?

On top, we have the Fruit Ring Mold with Dressing, perhaps the most nonspecific dish name in memory. Whether it contains more Mold than Fruit is for you to decide, of course. In the middle, Cheese Aspic. Also known as A Boil on a Clown's Arse. Below, a Cottage Cheese Log. Smeared on the walls, it yields enough light to read by.

Klan Batter was the only sauce banned by an act of Congress.

Only Tide gets your steaks whiter than white!

Or maybe it's that BBQ fire-starter, fresh-squeezed Siz! (See page 75.)

Off-White Sauce, for the more tasteful crowd. You know, no one thought twice about living under a sperm bank until their cooler broke and the pipes leaked.

Frankly, the Rapture took *everyone* by surprise that afternoon.

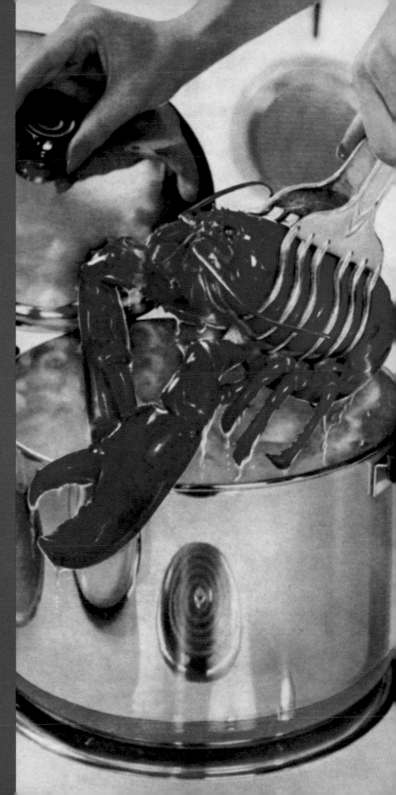

We end with a dish

that's no mystery at all. It's everyone's favorite screaming crustacean.

This picture might be titled "What Happens When You Don't Evolve." Take note, lobsters: Not only do you end up boiled to death and eaten by technologically advanced creatures with electric stoves and nice manicures, but they have special tongs just for you. So evolve, already. You have a lot of work to do. Or at least learn to shoot back; there must be millions of guns lying around the ocean floor from various wartime wrecks.

Recent studies suggest that lobsters don't really scream when dipped in scalding water; it's just the sound of escaping gases whistling through the shell. Too bad. Those are tremendously ugly creatures. If they were the size of Labrador retrievers, and you found one clawing at the bedroom window one night, you'd pass out from fear. The scream is a reassurance, really: That's one more lobster that won't evolve into something capable of breaking into the house. Pass the butter.

Fill Your Internal Organs with Meat! Meat! Meat!

Take a good long look at the zippy dish below, son, because it's the *last* scrap of veggies untainted by meat-proximity you're ever gonna see in this chapter.

It's an interesting dish: inflamed rabbit testes heaped on a layer of warm cucumbers, arranged on flatbread, and served on a bed of river-washed stones.

Now, on to the meat. Meat! And lots of it, in all its bloody glory! The last time this much chopped 'n' charred flesh was laid out in one place, it was a Roman battlefield. Meat!

MEAT! Let's begin. First, a lesson in how meat begins.

BREAST OF VEAL

Breast of veal. If you say so. Looks more like an aerial photograph of a geological formation, but if you say it's veal, then veal it is. (Sadist.)

BREAST OF LAMB

Breast of lamb. Again, we'll take your word for it. Nice how we can see the ribs. Makes you think you're eating fillet of runway model.

NECK OF LAMB

Neck of lamb. Well, now *hold on.* That's a lot of neck. Fillet of giraffe we'd accept, but lamb?

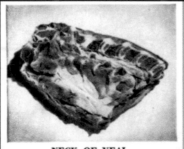

NECK OF VEAL.

Neck of veal. If you can see the indentations left by the spinal column, you know it's not a vegetable. But what becomes of these chunky sundered quadruped parts?

They're condensed

into portable portions and flavor-locked so the blood doesn't stain your Easter gloves. Now then: What delightful meals might we coax from this muscle chunk?

New protective CRYOVAC package locks in flavor...for keeps

The technical term preferred by chefs is "laced buttsteak." That's about the grumpiest piece of meat you'll see all day.

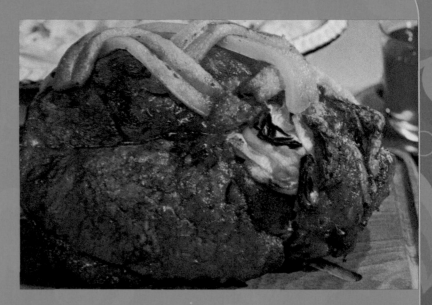

It's the latest craze— Glazed Ostrich Thigh à la paddleboat.

In the court of meat, this is the gavel. Verdict: Guilty—of being delicious!

What to do with all that peeled, sunburned skin you've been saving? Sprinkle over meat for a crunchtastic treat.

Mealtime hit—or severed limb?

And must they be mutually exclusive?

124

No question: severed limb.

The item in the background, incidentally, is a broiled catcher's mitt. Marinate for six years before cooking.

In the middle, Stone Cold Heaped Animal Cubes in Stone Cold Rice; on the left, Meat Entombed in Gelatin, Surrounded by Chopped Praying-Mantis Bodies. On the right, the Trojan Horse of meat-bearing entrées: the infamous Cabbage Stuffed to the Bursting Point with Spiced, Industrially Ground Flesh.

Imagine the look on a vegetarian's face: Ah. Ahhh. Finally, something from the bosom of the earth, kissed by the sun, nourished by the rain, a gentle thing that didn't scream in fear when the end came. Cut me a big slice of that cruelty-free lettuce, brother. Say—what's that inside? No! It cannot be!

Vegans will *punch* you if you serve them this.

Oh, admit it. You've always been curious to see what lies under an armadillo's shell.

Despite a massive publicity effort from Texaco, the "Motor-Oil Baste-O-Roast" technique never really caught on.

Upside: Ancient botanicals add a decorative twist, and make you wonder why they were banned by the Church. Downside: At some point in the recipe, you have to pledge your soul to Satan. High-altitude instructions: Stand on a chair while you pledge your soul to Satan.

Not many cuts of meat bear a
remarkable resemblance to the skull of a bloodhound, but this is one of them.

If the circular ring of Ketchup Jell-O or the Baked Pea Conclave don't thrill your guests, call their attention to the hand-formed meat-wads engaged in connubial relations with the zucchinis. Works every time.

Gangrene Brats require a good deal of advance preparation, but they're not particularly labor intensive. Just leave them alone for six months and then scrape off the flies.

Any
first-year

med student will tell you:
Yellow means a sinus
infection. Green is bronchial.

Context is everything.

Put it on a plate in the garden, and it's a fresh meal bursting with nature's goodness. Remove the plate and foliage, and it's something you'd find at the bottom of a portable john at an outdoor music festival.

From the
H. P. Lovecraft Necronomicookbook.

Behold the Slubgullionwich! An ancient sightless creature that has slumbered for untold millennia, a horrid embodiment of dispassionate evil whose awakening will usher in a day of ceaseless lamentations! Mothers, weeping, will offer up their young in the hopes that one might be spared! Fathers, despairing and prostrate, will pull out their entrails and beg for an easeful death!

Try it with the mustard.

It's a tough lesson for starry-eyed brides to learn, but meat is like, well, a starry-eyed bride: Upside down or right side up, it really doesn't matter.

Sweet-course idea inspires new main dish

Way No. 1   Meat Upside-Down Cake

4 tablespoons shortening
⅔ cup chopped onion
4 cups chopped cooked meat
1 cup milk

Prepared mustard to taste
Medium-thick brown gravy
2 cups Biscuit Short-Cut, page 5

Melt shortening in a frying pan, add onion and cook until tender. Season. Add the lean cooked meat, season to taste with mustard and moisten with gravy. Keep hot while preparing topping. To the Biscuit Short-Cut (use the richer kind, or chop in a little extra fat), add milk; combine mixture lightly to give a dough of "drop" consistency. Spread over hot meat and bake in hot oven, 425° to 450°, about 25 minutes. Turn out on heated serving dish, cut in wedges and serve with a hot medium-thick brown or tomato sauce—lots of it! Serves 6 rather hungry people.

SALMON CORN UPSIDE-DOWN CAKE. Prepare as above, but replace the meat and onion by a pound can of salmon, flaked and mixed with 2 cups drained kernel-type canned corn and chopped pimiento, finely-minced onion, salt and pepper to taste. Serve the baked upside-down cake with generous amount of medium-thick white sauce.

Context really is everything.

On a plate, it's supper. On your boulevard, it's a sign that the neighbor walked his six rottweilers this morning. Remarkably trained beasts, they are. The way they line up, it's a thing to behold. And then scoop up. Not that your neighbor scoops them up.

The tomatoes in the background remind us that Justice is blind.

Lucky Justice.

If you have difficulty lighting the charcoal in gusty conditions, seek a windbreak.

But who eats all this meat?

The all-American BBQ family! Let's turn the page
and take look at each of them.

Daddy's secret ingredient? Cigarette tobacco!

I told my son we would all be happy once he got rid of that awful woman. We're a family again. God's in his heaven, Sonny is home, and that bitch is in a barrel at the dump—sorry, I mean she went home to see her mother. Who was also a tramp. You could just tell where she got it from.

I don't know why Grandma made me wear this. She hates girls. In thirty years I will experience deep sexual confusion while watching *Miami Vice*. I wonder why Mommy left all her pretty things. Sometimes when I miss her I put them on.

Father, may I get a head start on my eating issues?

Sure, hon! Dig in. You'll get nothing but uncritical support from me, right up until the moment you exhibit secondary sex characteristics.

She looks nothing like her, thank God.

I wish I hadn't wet the bed last night.

And you won't wet it tonight, if you know what's good for you.

From the Cookbook Library

Selected Volumes of Fear and Loathing

★ ★ ★ ★ ★

Cooks have always cherished their recipe collections. In the Golden Age, the most important was the Grand Compendium, usually a battered, stained Betty Crocker volume that taught you everything from boiling water to carving up a rhino. The second variety: the "specific book," which had titles like *Meals for Two* or *Quick Brunches* or *Meat-Extending Miracles*. (You were supposed to put the book in the blender and fold the pulp into the chuck.) The finest example of the cookbook genre, however, was the promotional giveaway. It would have a name like *Fascinating Bologna!* and contain recipes on minced bologna pie, deviled bologna, bologna flan, bologna flambé, cold bologna soup, and so on. In the end you learned that the book had been prepared by Hogzoffle Bologna Company, or the American Bologna Council. You now find these books in every antique store—slick, colorful, delightful to behold, and utterly unused. Lucky for you, I've collected some of these artifacts from the junk drawer of time.

Who knew bananas were so complex, so daunting, so mysterious, that they needed an entire book to explain them to the public? "How to serve them!" What a novel concept. Heretofore people had just set them on the counter and had a good old-fashioned "ripening race." I bet on the long one to turn black first! You're on, sis. Let's synchronize our sundials and let the fun begin!

Perhaps the book was intended to subtly reinforce the phallocentric paradigm of the patriarchy, reminding women that these provocatively shaped items were meant to be served. Not questioned, not doubted, not insulted with an endless series of remarks about how your sister's bananas made more money. If so, the book does a poor job, since it's all about chopping them into slices or mashing them into paste.

BANANAS...how to serve them

Our first recipe. Broiled Abominable Snowman Penis.

Who likes bananas?

Well, gosh, just about everyone. Glamorous, desirable girls who seriously believed this photo shoot would lead to motion picture work enjoy bananas, and so do sexless, tooth-bereft archetypes of age and decay who look at you as though you'd just proposed a vinegar enema.

KEEP that slender figure — eat bananas. They're nourishing and satisfying and low in fat content. An average-sized banana contains about 120 calories.

OLD FOLKS find fully ripe bananas a pleasant, satisfying treat—easy to chew, easy to digest, low in protein, high in quick food energy.

BABIES THRIVE on fully ripe bananas, mashed or strained and fed with a spoon—one of the earliest solid foods fed the Dionne quintuplets.

Babies love 'em—especially commercially exploited Canadian freak-litter babies.

IN THE 'TEENS the right foods keep energy up to par, eyes bright, skin clear. There's quick food energy in fully ripe bananas, plus vitamins and minera's.

Teens love 'em, although girls who ate them on the first date got a permanent reputation. If guys ate them and loved it, they kept it to themselves.

This photo originally appeared in a popular mail-order instruction pamphlet, "How to Subdue Women."

Heh Heh Heh

She's moving toward the fruit—heh—oh please let her pick up the bananas.

Heh

SHE DID SHE DID SHE *DID* PICK UP THE BANANAS! . . .

Okay, stay calm . . .

Heh

She's coming over to buy them—get ready.

Okay, SHOW HER MISTER BANANA!

Aw, why do they always gotta scream?

HOW TO BUY BANANAS — Buy bananas by the "hand" or cluster at the stage of ripeness you find them in the store. (They average about two to three bananas to a pound.)

SALAD FORTUNES

Told-Free

A long life and a merry one to Salad-Servers . . .

Predictions

YOUR SALADS WILL BRING YOU **FAME**

The secret to long life and happiness?

According to the salad fortune-teller, the secret isn't eating salads, but serving them. As for the predictions, our seer doesn't exactly hit these out of the park. Two people have been granted fame by salads: Cobb and Caesar.

YOUR SALADS WILL BRING YOU **MONEY**

But you will lose it all in the Romaine Panic of '38.

YOUR SALADS WILL BRING YOU **PLEASURE**

The spirits tell me your arrangement of spinach and shredded carrots will produce an orgasm that curls your toes so hard they will have to be straightened with a hot bath and a pliers. The spirits never lie!

One of the tried-and-true

ways to make Mrs. Middle America feel 14 percent better about slaving over a hellish oven was the celebrity recipe book—in this case, a compendium of tips from Hollywood stars and rich society widows who hadn't baked anything since they helped the servants make cookies in second grade. This book contained private recipes from such noted bakers as Clark Gable and Joan Crawford, each of whom had found fascinating ways to incorporate Bisquick into their glamorous lives. Turn the page for more.

LET THE STARS SHOW YOU

CLARK GABLE · COUNTESS FAL de ST. PHALLE · MAY ROBSON · MRS. THOMAS J. HILLIARD · DICK POWELL · NELL B. NICHOLS

HOW TO TAKE A TRICK A DAY WITH BISQUICK

PRICE 25¢

AS TOLD TO *Betty Crocker*

BY SCREEN STARS, SOCIETY STARS, HOME STARS AND STAR HOMEMAKING EDITORS

See? The stars are just like us. Aside from the money, fame, licentious private lives, and publicists. And while we're on our way to Miss Crawford's trailer, pal, let me tell you how we play things here. The folks back home eat Bisquick and go to the movies. They like to know the stars eat Bisquick too. Sure, you might have a quote from Miss Crawford's maid who says her boss threw a scone at her head because it tasted like it was made from circus sawdust, and demanded that she run down to the Brown Derby and pick up some Parker Rolls and a fifth of gin while she was at it, but there's truth, and there's a bigger truth, if you know what I mean. And the bigger truth is, you ain't Louella Parsons.

JOAN CRAWFORD

Metro-Goldwyn-Mayer's Star of

"I LIVE MY LIFE"

● in addition to her fame as an actress, is known in Hollywood for her clever home management. She plans all her own menus, including those for her Smart Dinners, such as the one given below.

★

Variety of Hors d'Oeuvres   Bisquick Cheese Straws
Cream of Lettuce Soup
Broccoli with Hollandaise
Mixed Grill of English Mutton Chop with Kidney,
Bacon and Mushrooms
Chutney   Mangoes   Whole Wheat Bisquicks
Potatoes on Half Shell   Avocado Salad
Platter of Fresh Fruits, Glacèd
(*Whole Pears, Peaches and Apricots with clusters of Grapes, Watermelon and Honey Dew Balls, Cherries*)
Fresh Coconut Cake   Bonbons   Coffee

See Bisquick recipes on pages 36 to 41.

Jug-eared cuss,

wasn't he? Nevertheless, Mr. Gable was correct: Men do invariably prefer the Hunter's Breakfast, also known as the Guy Who Was Up Until 3 A.M. Playing Xbox Breakfast, or the Hungover Trucker's Breakfast, or the Insurance Salesman Who Hasn't Made a Sale This Month and Is Sitting at Denny's Wondering Where Life Is Taking Him, What with a Wife He Hardly Knows Anymore and a Child Whose Cheerful Face Has Been Replaced by Sullen Teen Goth-Mask, and Now He Has This Pain in His Chest That Won't Go Away Anymore Breakfast. In short: If the subject in question has testicles, he prefers this breakfast. Although you can skip the fruit.

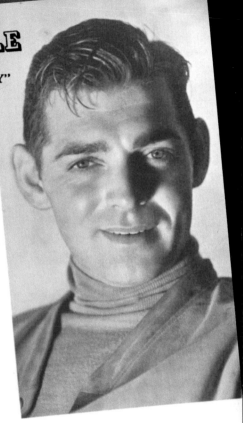

CLARK GABLE
Metro-Goldwyn-Mayer's Star of "MUTINY ON THE BOUNTY"

● a great outdoors enthusiast and a skilled hunter . . . finds that men invariably prefer this Hunters' Breakfast—

Fruit in Season
Cereal with Cream and Sugar
Fried Eggs and Bacon
Bisquick Griddle Cakes with Maple Syrup
Coffee

● Dr. A. E. DuBarry of Lyons, Montana, an explorer and prospector who has followed the lonely trail through desert wastes and mountains for a lifetime, says: "Bisquick is a wonderful help for the out-of-door man, explorer, hunter, and prospector. My pardner and myself are prospectors and we may truly say your Bisquick certainly does perfectly solve the problem of quick bread in camp. I have prepared Bisquicks in the camp stove, over hot coals, in a Dutch oven, between two frying pans, and I may say that it has never failed me! Bisquick is ideal for the camper any place, for quickly prepared and delicious camp dishes . . . We made two lucky strikes in succession—the use of Bisquick and the discovery of our mine!"

31

One of the more Bisquick-intensive meals in the book. It's a Southern Plantation Supper! How Southern Plantation is it? *This* Southern Plantation: It's Mammy Lou approved!

BING CROSBY
Paramount's Singing Star of
"TWO FOR TONIGHT" *and* "ANYTHING GOES"

● is crazy about his wife's

Southern Plantation Supper

★

Chicken Fried in Batter
(Bisquick)
Corn Fritters (Bisquick)
Candied Sweet Potatoes
Tomato Sections Lettuce
Spoon Bread
Chocolate Ice Box Cake
Coffee

Mammy Lou says: "Laws, Honey, it don't take no time at all. I use Bisquick batter to fry my chicken in, and folks tell me my chicken has the real old Southern flavor."

13

Golf Club Buffet Supper
Hot Roast of Beef   Escalloped Potatoes
Banana Fritters (Bisquick)   Platter of Cold Meats
Corn and Tomatoes au Gratin
Green Beans   Cabbage Slaw
Individual Molds of Fruit Salad
Shrimp a la Newburg on hot Bisquicks
Rolls   Orange Bread (Bisquick)
Peppermint Chocolate Angel Food Dessert   Coffee

See Bisquick recipes on pages 36 to 41

Mammy Lou says: "Laws, Honey, it don't take no time at all. I use Bisquick batter to fry my chicken in, and folks tell me my chicken has the real old Southern flavor."

13

"Rich and flaky."

That might not be a direct quote, but no doubt accurately reflects Miss Davis's general opinion of the product. There is also no evidence she used the term "London Buns" to refer to romantic interests.

"Bisquick makes rich, flaky Hunt Club Sandwiches."

BETTE DAVIS
Warner Brothers' Star of
"FRONT PAGE WOMAN"

● acclaimed for her fine interpretation of emotional roles, keeps her love of the simple homey things of her New England background.

TEA SUGGESTIONS

Bisquick Scones
Jam or Jelly   Plum Cake
Tea

•

Jelly Tea Biscuits   Tea
Lemon Cookies

•

Watercress Sandwiches
London Buns   Tea

•

Brown Bread Sandwiches
Marmalade
Bisquick Pinwheels
Shortbread   Tea

•

"Bisquick makes rich, flaky Hunt Club Sandwiches."

Bette Davis enjoying Ham Bisquicks for afternoon tea in her dressing room.

Hunt Club Sandwiches (Bisquick)
Fruit Salad   Tea or Coffee   Tiny Cakes

Olive Sandwiches   Lemon Bread (Bisquick)
Variety of Cookies   Tea

Broiled Crabmeat Sandwiches
Ginger Waffles (Bisquick) with Cream Cheese
Tea or Coffee

(See Bisquick recipes on pages 36 to 41.)

25

153

LONI ANDERSON'S FETTUCINI A LA ROSS

1 lb. fettucini
1 pint whipping cream or half and half
¼ lb. lean prosciutto or baked ham, cut in thin slices
2 oz. butter
¼ tsp. sage, crushed
⅛ tsp. red pepper - pepperoncini
⅓ cup Marsala wine
¼-½ cup Parmesan cheese

Fill spaghetti pot ¾ full of water and add one tsp. salt. Bring to boil. While waiting for water to boil, melt butter in large pan, then add prosciutto or ham and saute for about 5 minutes. Add spices and Marsala and mix thoroughly, allowing liquid to evaporate just a little. Lower the heat to simmer. When water boils, add fettucini. Bring water back to boil and cook 6-8 minutes, making sure fettucini doesn't get too soggy. While fettucini is boiling, add cream to sauce, stirring constantly and bringing sauce to a boil so mixture thickens enough to coat the fettucini. Drain fettucini, but do not rinse. Add to sauce, then add Parmesan cheese and toss together until sauce and cheese coat each strand of fettucini. Turn onto a large platter and serve with salad and red wine.

JAMES CAAN'S KIDNEY STEW

1½ lbs. veal or lamb kidneys
4 T. salad oil, divided in half
¼ cup yellow onion, chopped
1 clove garlic, pressed
1 T. tomato catsup
1 tsp. original Worcestershire sauce
  salt to taste
  freshly ground black pepper to taste
⅓ cup brandy or kirsch
  hot, cooked potatoes, peeled
  fresh minced parsley

Remove all of the outer membrane and most of the fat, central fat and white tubes from kidneys. Wash kidneys carefully in running water. Soak them in well-salted water about 30 minutes, changing water once (to remove strong flavor). Mean while heat 2 T. salad oil over low heat, adding onion and garlic. Cook, stirring, until onion is lightly golden. Remove kidneys from water and dry well on absorbent towelling. Slice kidney into½ inch slices.

In separate skillet, brown kidneys quickly in remaining salad oil unitl meat begins to turn white. Add sauteed kidneys to onion-garlic mixture. Stir in tomato catsup, Worcestershire sauce, and salt and pepper to taste. Simmer over low heat for a few minutes.

Pour brandy into a ladle that is hot. Pour heated spirits over kidneys and flame. Do not flame longer than 1 minute or kidneys will toughen. Serve at once with hot, peeled potatoes, garnished with fresh minced parsley. Serves 4.

6

Eventually the definition of "Star" changed.

Tastes became a bit more democratic, and the standards seem to have sagged somewhat. Proof? Sure: Here are some Famous Person Recipes from the waning hours of the 1970s.

Put water in the pot and bring it to a *boil?* That's the sort of family secret, passed down from generation to generation, that make the difference between a cook and a *chef.* Bet Loni's grandma gave her a hard look after this was published. *You are dead to me! Dead!*

James Caan's Kidney Stew:

Runner-up in the 1977 "Least Appetizing Four Words" competition. First place went to "Redd Foxx's Rump Roast."

MRS. ALAN ALDA'S PEPPER STEAK

2 lbs. top-grade steak, cut 1-inch thick
2 T. peppercorns
   salt to taste
3 T. butter
1 T. fresh parsley, minced
   few drops oil from pressed garlic
3 T. beef broth
3 T. Cognac
   watercress or parsley for garnish

Dry steaks with a paper towel. Crush peppercorns coarsely with a rolling pin or with a mortar and pestle. Rub and press crushed peppercorns into both sides of steaks using your fingers and the heel of your hand. Let steaks stand at room temperature for several hours, or until the meat absorbs the flavor of the pepper.

Pre-heat grill. Broil steaks 3-4 inches from heat until brown; turn and grill on reverse side about 5 minutes longer for very rare meat; longer for well-done steak. Transfer to heated platter at once and salt to taste.

Pour cooking juices from broiler pan into a small skillet, adding butter, parsley, garlic, beef broth and Cognac. Cook over medium heat until sauce is reduced in volume by ½. Pour sauce over steak. Garnish with watercress. Serve at once. Serves 4.

JOHN DAVIDSON'S "THE THING"

3 lbs. lean ground chuck
1 T. butter
1 medium yellow onion, peeled and finely chopped
1 large green pepper, chopped
3 large stalks celery, minced
1 can (3 oz.) mushrooms, sliced and drained
¼ tsp. freshly ground pepper
½ tsp. salt
¼ tsp. garlic powder
1 scant tsp. curry powder
1½ cups marinara or spaghetti sauce, canned
1 can (1 lb.) basil-flavored Italian-style plum tomatoes
2½ cups elbow macaroni, cooked

Saute beef in butter in a large stock pot with onion, green pepper, celery, mushrooms, salt and pepper. Cook over low heat, stirring with a wooden spoon until meat browns and vegetables are transparent. Mixture should have a 'loose' consistency. Add garlic powder, curry powder, marinara sauce and tomatoes. Cook over low heat, uncovered, 10 minutes, stirring often to prevent sticking. Add cooked macaroni and heat thoroughly. Serve along or with tossed green salad and garlic bread. Serves 8-10.

7

As a sign of your moral seriousness, do not use a laugh track while making this meal.

Also, it may seem like it's about steak and the timeless nature of men and women exposed to pepper, but it's really about Vietnam.

Thank God for "The," or hostesses across America would invite everyone to carve up John Davidson's Thing. As recipes go, it's cool; it's hip; it's layered, feathered, parted in in the middle. Canned sauce? Got it. Make sure that pepper's freshly ground; chicks dig it when you whip out that big piano leg and grind off a hit. And you need a loose mixture; an uptight mixture would *totally* ruin the vibe.

"And How to Avoid Them"

would be more accurate; "How Not to Smack Into the Wall While Running Out of the Room" would be better. It's difficult to imagine why the animals are dancing. What's the occasion? "They're going to eat our bray-ains, they're going to eat our bray-ains! They're going to mince our thyroid glands and serve them with some gray-ains!"

Variety Meats **THEIR APPEARANCE AND HOW TO COOK THEM**

SWEETBREADS

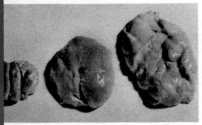

Broil, Fry, Braise, Cook in Liquid

TONGUES

Cook in Liquid

BRAINS

Broil, Fry, Braise, Cook in Liquid

HEARTS

Braise, Cook in Liquid

LIVERS

Beef, Pork: Roast, Braise, Fry
Veal, Lamb: Broil, Panbroil, Fry

KIDNEYS

Beef, Pork: Braise, Cook in Liquid
Veal, Lamb: Broil, Panbroil, Braise,
Cook in Liquid

24

Courtesy of the National Live Stock and Meat Board

SIMMERED BRAINS

1. Wash beef, veal, lamb or pork brains in cold water.
2. Soak ½ hour in salted water, allowing 1 tablespoon salt per quart water.
3. Remove membrane.
4. Place in pan; add water to cover, 1 teaspoon salt, 1 tablespoon lemon juice or vinegar for each quart water.
5. Cover; simmer over low heat 15–20 minutes.
6. Drain; drop into cold water; drain again.
7. Serve with Mushroom, Tomato or Butter Sauce.
8. Allow four servings per pound.

SAUTÉED BRAINS

1. Prepare Simmered Brains.
2. Dip into beaten egg, then in fine dry crumbs or corn meal.
3. Sauté in butter in fry pan until brown.

BROILED BRAINS

1. Prepare Simmered Brains.
2. Brush with melted butter.
3. Broil 10–15 minutes, turning occasionally.
4. Serve with lemon wedges, broiled bacon, broiled tomatoes or Beet and Horseradish Relish.

Simmered, sauteed, or broiled—your options are endless.

Serve with beets, because little finicky kids want nothing more than Broiled Brains with Beets.

If the kid balks, point out that you removed the membrane.

SCOTCH HEART PATTIES

1¼ pounds beef heart
1 medium onion
½ cup quick-cooking rolled oats
1½ teaspoons salt
⅛ teaspoon pepper
All-purpose flour
2 tablespoons fat
1½ cups water

Wash and trim heart and remove large tubes, excess fat, and blood vessels. Force heart and onion through food grinder, using fine blade. Add oats, salt, and pepper. Let stand for at least 30 minutes. Then, with well-floured hands, shape mixture into 8 thin patties, coating each patty with flour. Brown slowly on both sides in hot fat. Remove patties and keep hot. Blend 1½ tablespoons flour into drippings remaining in skillet. Add water and cook until thickened. Season with additional salt and pepper if necessary. Serve as a sauce with the patties. Makes 4 servings.

After the family tires of broiled brain, move on to the heart. Make

some Scotch Heart Patties, also known as Braveheart Burgers. First, remove large tubes, set aside for later use (for Chest Cheese, perhaps), then force heart through food grinder.

Scotch Heart Patties, when hooked up to a small electrical charge, pulse spasmodically, which makes them both delicious and educational. Let Dad have the first stab! Fill them with ketchup, strike them with your fist, and simulate the miracle of circulation!

When first we learn that a thing called "head cheese" exists, and we're told that half the term is inaccurate, most of us are pulling for "head." It's like getting a bowl of Toe Pudding. *Please let there be no toes*, please *let there be no toes.*

Alas, head cheese is mostly head. And not even the choice cuts of the head. As the recipe states, it's made up of cheeks, noses, and "underlips." Sometimes feet are added, especially if people had previously complained that your head cheese wasn't footy enough.

You could buy it at the store, but why? After a hard day getting tongue-whipped by Mr. Drysdale, nothing puts a smile on Hubby's face like the aroma of fresh-scoured pig skull. The ingredients are easy enough to assemble; wine is provided in the recipe so you can fortify yourself while conducting the nauseating assembly. When you have finished boiling the stripped horror-meats, press them into a mold, chill, serve, and apologize.

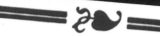

HEAD CHEESE—Head cheese is a well-seasoned cold cut made of the edible parts of a calf's or a pig's head such as the cheeks, snouts, and underlips, to which sometimes brains, hearts, tongues, and feet are added. The meat is boiled, stripped from the bones, skinned, cut into pieces, and seasoned with onions, herbs, and spices. Then it is put into a mold and pressed into a firm, jellied mass.

Head cheese is named so misleadingly because, at one time, cheese was added to the meat. It is available in food stores, as are other cold cuts, but it can also be made at home.

Head cheese is used in Scandinavian smörgåsbord, in French hors-d'oeuvre, and in German, Swiss, and Austrian sandwiches. Every country where farm people butcher meat has its own version of head cheese.

Squirrel Pie:

Remember—an important part of this dish is squirrel. Accept no substitutes.

SQUIRREL PIE

1 squirrel	Biscuits
3 tablespoons flour	2 cups flour
$\frac{1}{2}$ tablespoon minced parsley	4 teaspoons baking powder
1 teaspoon salt	$\frac{1}{2}$ teaspoon salt
$\frac{1}{8}$ teaspoon pepper	$\frac{1}{4}$ cup fat
$\frac{1}{2}$ cup fresh cut mushrooms	$\frac{2}{3}$ cup milk
2 cups stock or milk	

Disjoint and cut squirrel into 2 or 3 pieces. Cover with water and cook 1 hour. Remove meat from bones in large pieces. Add flour, parsley, salt, pepper and mushrooms to the stock. Cook until it thickens (5 to 10 minutes). Add the meat and mix well. Pour into baking dish.

Make the biscuits by sifting the flour, baking powder and salt together. Cut in the fat and add the milk. Stir until all dry ingredients are moistened. Roll only enough to make it fit the baking dish.

Place dough on meat in baking dish. Bake in moderate oven (350°F.) until dough is golden brown. (30 to 40 minutes.) 6-8 servings.

Smothered Muskrat:

How you smother it is up to you, but most people use an old blanket. Avoid those store-bought presoaked predisjointed muskrats, if you can.

SMOTHERED MUSKRAT AND ONIONS

1 muskrat	3 tablespoons fat
$1\frac{1}{2}$ teaspoons salt	3 large onions, sliced
$\frac{1}{4}$ teaspoon paprika	1 cup sour cream
$\frac{1}{2}$ cup flour	

Soak muskrat overnight in salted water (1 tablespoon salt to 1 quart water). Drain, disjoint and cut up. Season with 1 teaspoon salt, paprika, roll in flour and fry in fat until browned. Cover muskrat with onions, sprinkle onions with ½ teaspoon salt. Pour in the cream. Cover skillet tightly and simmer for 1 hour. Serves 4.

ROAST BEAVER

1 small or medium-sized beaver	sliced onions
baking soda	bacon

Remove all surface fat. Cover meat with a weak solution of soda and water. (1 tsp. soda to 1 qt. water.) Boil 10 minutes and drain. Cover beaver with bacon and onions and roast until tender.

FRIED BEAVER

Use a small beaver cut into pieces. Remove fat and soak overnight in cold water—drain. Cook in a small amount of water until tender then fry with bacon and seasoning salt. Try some hickory-smoked seasoning salt on this.

Roast Beaver:

As you can tell, the majority of the flavor is beaver-specific.

Fried Beaver:

This presumes you have beavers of various sizes on hand from which to choose. Don't we all?

Presenting: Nondescript fried meat heaped in the traditional jumble, garnished with the usual rabbit food. But what is it?

Why, rabbit food! Literally.

In addition to the above cut-up frozen packages, some stores offer PEL-FREEZ whole tender young rabbits.

Yes, well, so do most, bus stations men's rooms.

If you wish, you can blend the meat into this: Rabbit Loaf. Bunny Hunk. Slab o' Fluffy. A "Bugs Wedge." A frame from Peter Rabbit's MRI. Mr. McGregor's Revenge. Just tell everyone it's Hammer-Stunned Veal, and they'll be less horrified. Or direct their attention to the the clever way you've organized the rabbit organs into an ice-cream cone, complete with springtimey "marrow clouds."

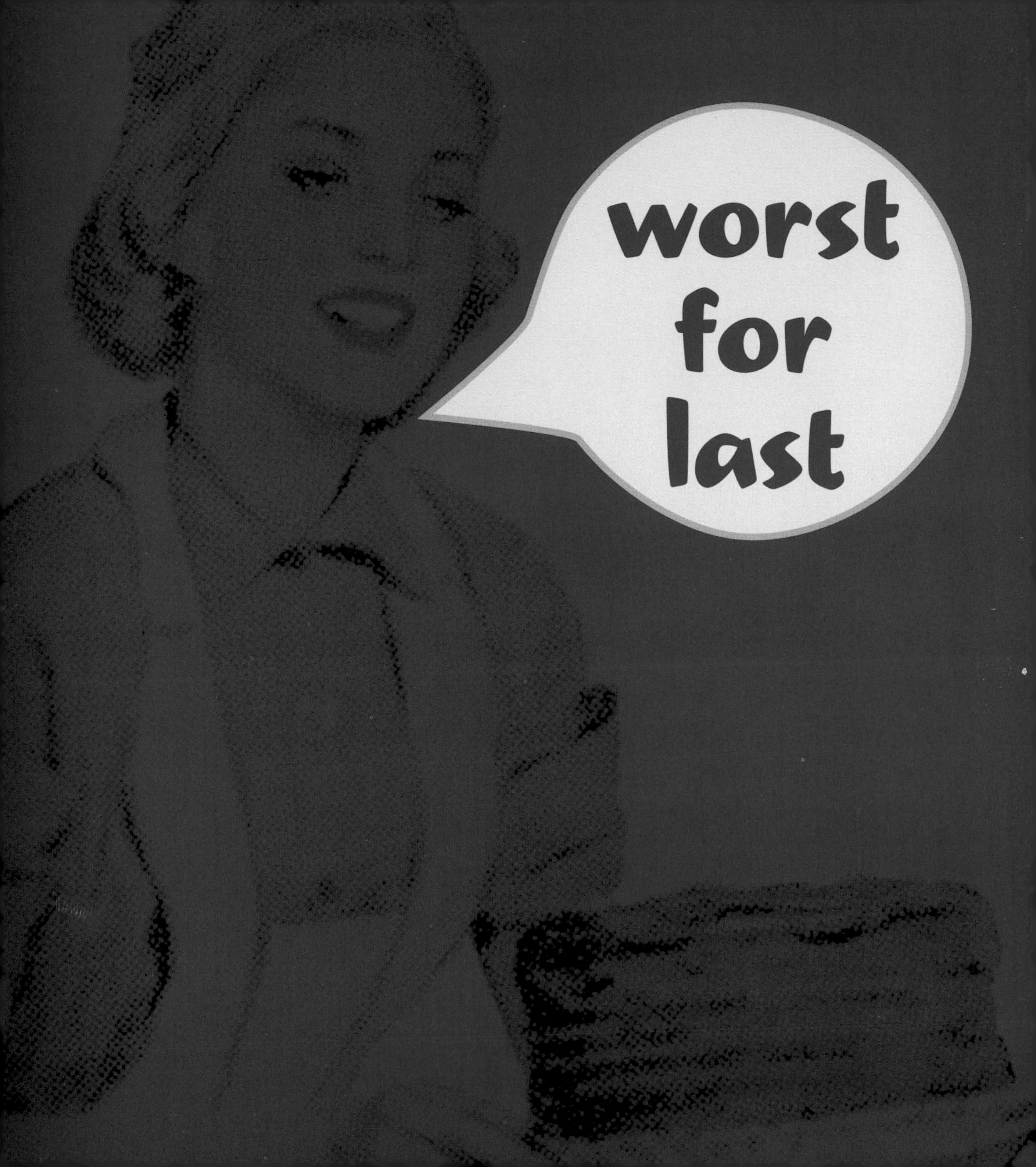
worst for last

End on a (Sickeningly) Sweet Note

I know what you're thinking: There's only so much damage you can do with desserts. In the times of culinary catastrophe we are examining, people simply did not stand for undue innovation with dessert. Nowadays you can get away with mango-kissed carob-coated ahi ahi sliced three microns thin and drizzled with condensed Cointreau fumes, but back then you had to offer up the tried and true standards.

We had four varieties of ice cream when I was growing up: vanilla, chocolate, strawberry, and Neapolitan, which was all of the above combined. If you had sophisticated relatives with Continental airs, you might encounter spumoni, which was noted for the moist unattractive nodules of something-or-other embedded in the dessert. Nuts, raisins, Rocky Mountain oysters, who knew. At some point French vanilla ice cream was introduced, and this turned the dessert paradigm on its head, much as the rumors of something called "cheesecake" had sent homemakers frantically paging through *Woman's Day* to find out how this peculiar confection might be made.

The following are attempts to give Mom something to serve besides ice cream. To ensure success, ice cream is occasionally involved.

And . . . Exceptionally unnecessary!

Today, anyway. The modern supermarket has six miles of ice cream, in all possible flavors. But in the early fifties, you could make your own grape ice cream, thanks to Ten-B-Low, a superdense ice cream concentrate. You may ask: How is it possible to concentrate ice cream? Simple: the Ten-B-Low company used a secret technology reversed from the Roswell UFO crash, and embedded small superchilled nanotubes in the body of the can, compressing the space between the individual atoms while compensating for the nominal increase in heat arising from the extra density.

Or, it was a can of dried chemicals. In either case, the end result was ice cream the color of a prize-fighter's eye socket.

The unexpected crunchy
texture of Light Bulb Flan.
   Note: In California, you
must substitute compact
fluorescents by 2009.

The cross section of Clown Mountain reveals a rich inner core of lava, ready to erupt with deliciousness!

Tasty as it certainly looks, you have to wonder about portion size. I mean, that's thirty cubic inches of dessert, minimum. Best not to cut it open before guests arrive, or they might suspect it's actually nine pounds of margarine over a pile of raw hamburger.

When Count Chocula took over Candyland, he had all his opponents impaled and displayed outside the castle. It had the effect of discouraging dissent, as he knew it would.

Forty minutes into Johnny's party,

the peyote smoothies finally began to take hold.

168

THE ICE OASIS is a grand new, brand-new idea for serving an elegant fresh or canned ICE JET fruit cocktail. Drain fruit thoroughly first, then *mix* with crushed ice.

Pack this ice-fruit mixture tightly into an ice bucket. Then invert the bucket on a deep plate of crushed ice. Garnish with red cherries, add pineapple, nuts or cookies, served in fluted paper cups or on tiny doilies, to the edges of the serving plate. A small fork should be included at each place setting for plucking the deliciously chilled fruit from its sparkling ice nest. By rubbing various colors of food coloring over the pineapple slices you can make them "snap" out.

The Ice Oasis is light and refreshing enough for a mid-afternoon snack and perfect for bridge or shower entertaining.

That's a lot of work
for six lousy cherries.

What is this? A closer
examination indicates it's some sort of dirt
pie with creamed lettuce frosting. The
tomatoes warn you off, though: This cannot
possibly be dessert, unless you're in some
alternate universe where roasted Key Lime
Pie is the main course, and dessert consists
of gravy-drizzled asparagus. Scientists
admit that such a universe may exist, if
superstring theory is correct, and all
possible permutations of our current reality
exist on other dimensional planes. But even
in those planes, kids won't touch this.

Since the main ingredient is cranberries, it's safe to assume these could be called *Crandles*. For extra fun, hide a cherry bomb in one. Not recommended for homes with flocked, hard-to-clean wallpaper.

"Gosh, I love coffee—if only it wasn't a hot liquid, but came in a cold, jiggly cube I could eat with a fork!" Here you go, served with a side of espresso. Just look at the size of that dish! Your heart would wear a groove in your sternum by the time you were halfway through.

**The only time
you get color
combinations**
like this is when you let three-
year-olds dress themselves.

There's a chance it could be
pistachio. There's also a chance
it could be coagulated body
paint from a '56 Chevy.

When serving chilled albino brains for dessert, always include one of those "hypnotism coins" sold in old comic books, so you can convince your guests this is actual tapioca, and not something a coroner was weighing in a pan six hours ago.

It's supposed to be a cranberry-based dessert, but you suspect they used the same picture for "Calf Hearts with Hollandaise Sauce."

Cranberry Blossoms

A HAPPY
ENDING TO
ANY MEAL

Kellogg's

KAFFEE HAG
COFFEE

97% Caffeine-*Free*
100% Flavor-*ful*

6619   Printed in U. S. A.

A *final note.* When your author was a bartender, "Kaffee Hag" was the name we gave to the weird ancient post-grad students who nursed a cup of java for six hours and smoked thirty-six Merit cigarettes while watching the afternoon soaps. "Kaffee Hag," as it turns out, was also a pseudo-coffee beverage. Even in the days of the Depression people were worried about caffeine, and you can see why—with structural unemployment of 30 percent and Hitler on the way, who wants to spend more time awake than necessary? Of course this couple has no cares, since they're loaded. But there's something else going on here—it's as if she just said, *"Oh I think being tied up would be fun, in a naughty sort of way,"* and he cannot *believe* his luck. Six years of marriage, and it comes out at a dinner party.

Kaffee Hag! A happy ending to *every* meal.